magical
forest fairy crafts
THROUGH THE SEASONS

Make 25 Enchanting Forest Fairies, Gnomes & More from Simple Supplies

LENKA VODICKA-PAREDES and ASIA CURRIE

FunStitch
STUDIO
an imprint of C&T Publishing

PUBLISHER: Amy Marson

CREATIVE DIRECTOR: Gailen Runge

ACQUISITIONS EDITOR: Roxane Cerda

MANAGING EDITOR: Liz Aneloski

EDITOR: Monica Gyulai

TECHNICAL EDITOR: Linda Johnson

COVER/BOOK DESIGNER: April Mostek

PRODUCTION COORDINATOR: Tim Manibusan

PRODUCTION EDITOR: Jennifer Warren

ILLUSTRATOR: Aliza Shalit

PHOTO ASSISTANT: Mai Yong Vang

STYLE PHOTOGRAPHY by Lucy Glover and
INSTRUCTIONAL PHOTOGRAPHY by Mai Yong Vang
of C&T Publishing, Inc., unless otherwise noted

Published by FunStitch Studio, an imprint of C&T Publishing, Inc., P.O. Box 1456, Lafayette, CA 94549

Library of Congress Cataloging-in-Publication Data

Names: Vodicka-Paredes, Lenka, 1972- author. | Currie, Asia, 1962- author.

Title: Magical forest fairy crafts through the seasons : make 25 enchanting forest fairies, gnomes & more from simple supplies / Lenka Vodicka-Paredes and Asia Currie.

Description: Lafayette, CA : FunStitch Studio, an imprint of C&T Publishing, Inc., [2018] | Includes bibliographical references.

Identifiers: LCCN 2017053526 | ISBN 9781617456619 (soft cover)

Subjects: LCSH: Dollmaking--Juvenile literature. | Nature craft--Juvenile literature. | Fairies in art--Juvenile literature. | Handicraft for children--Juvenile literature. | Sewing--Juvenile literature.

Classification: LCC TT175 .V63 2018 | DDC 745.592/21--dc23

LC record available at https://lccn.loc.gov/2017053526

Printed in China

10 9 8 7 6 5 4 3 2 1

DEDICATION

For my children, Miranda, Trevyn, and Gwynna, and my granddaughter, Hadi.
To my husband, Gabriel, for making me meals while I worked in Fairyland.   *With love from Asia*

For Anika, Ian, and Mila for believing in Fairyland.
To my husband, Giovanni, for supporting my fairy adventures.   *With love from Lenka*

Acknowledgments

Thank you to A Child's Dream (achildsdream.com) for collecting wonderful resources for fairy crafters. Your store is a wonderful family operation that continues to inspire us with dreamy felt and quality craft supplies.

Many thanks to Kathleen Rushall at the Andrea Brown Literary Agency for being our tireless champion. Magic is real!

To our fairy-crafting community: You are creative and fun and lovely. We appreciate you crafting with us through the years. We are especially grateful to all the kids who share their imagination and excitement with us. Thank you for making the world a better place—one fairy craft at a time!

contents

basic fairy family   24

spring   50

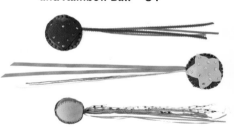

Welcome to the Forest

Forest Fairy Crafts

Fairies Want to Share the Year with You!

The forest has been busy since we wrote our first book, *Forest Fairy Crafts*. We continued to make magical fairies and crafts, and we learned that fairies love all the seasons and the way the forest changes during the year. They enjoy dressing up in festive outfits, finding new nature friends (like foxes), and creating toys. Fairies adore gifts and delight in giving.

Magical Forest Fairy Crafts Through the Seasons has all the information you need to make beautiful and fun fairies and sewing projects. Though this book is great for those who are new to fairy making, you will find new ideas if you already have *Forest Fairy Crafts*. We discovered new ways to decorate crafts, including cutting fancy edges (page 21) and sewing with the manta ray stitch (page 16). We made new fairies, including the bride and groom fairies (page 78). But we have a few returning favorites, such as flower fairies (page 53).

Fairy crafts make great decorations. They also make great gifts. Consider spreading joy by donating fairies to a local children's hospital or a retirement home. The fairies and critters in the forest want to make the world a better place—you can help!

Invite an adult to craft with you. They may need a good reason to slow down, and they will enjoy spending time with you. Or invite a younger child to craft with you. Then *you* become the teacher.

Photo by Lenka Vodicka-Paredes

We are so excited to open the forest to friends again. We hope you enjoy the new crafts!

Which Project Will You Make?

Choose crafts that inspire you. To make it easier to select, we've labeled them as *simple*, *fancy*, or *tricky*. If you don't have a lot of time or are new to Fairyland, start with the simple ones and build your skills. Keep sewing and learning!

simple These crafts are quick and a good place to start. You may want an adult to help you with the first ones you make. Then you will be ready to make them on your own. Be creative and have fun!

fancy Fancy projects may need more time and patience; ask for help along the way. Add more stitches and decorations. These projects are worth the extra effort!

tricky Tricky projects are fun to make with a helper. They may involve more pieces or steps and may feel challenging at first. Be kind to yourself as you work. The finished craft will be amazing!

Photo by Lenka Vodicka-Paredes

TIPS for Adult Helpers
Grown-ups can find great ideas on how to help kids make these crafts in Notes for Adults (page 130).

Things You Will Need

The projects in this book are made with simple supplies available at craft stores (some supplies can even be found in the forest!). Felt, sewing needles, crochet thread, chenille stems, wood beads, yarn, and decorations such as buttons and sequins are often used for fairy making. Collect your supplies in a handy basket or box so it's easy to find them whenever you want to go to Fairyland.

Needles

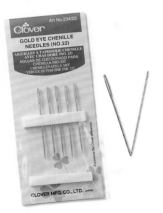

Craft and sewing stores have different needles for different types of sewing. You want a needle with a large eye that can fit larger threads. Very young sewists (under five years of age) may benefit from a tapestry needle that has a blunt tip. These needles may not be sharp enough to go through high-quality felt, however. If you are using beads, try putting the needle through the bead before starting a project to check that the needle will fit. Choose a needle that feels comfortable to you, keeping in mind that smaller needles can be trickier to control.

Thread

The thread that we use the most is *crochet thread size 10*, which may be found near the yarn aisle in craft stores. Crochet thread is thin but strong and doesn't tangle too easily. It comes in many colors, including mixed (or *variegated*) colors. We also use *embroidery floss* by separating the threads into three strands. For hanging ornaments or adding whiskers or antennae, we use *perle cotton thread sizes 3 and 5*. Feel free to mix and match threads however you like in your projects—that's what makes them yours!

Felt

Usually sold in precut rectangles, felt is available in a few different varieties, including wool felt, wool blends, and craft felt. For keepsakes, wool felt and wool blends come in rich colors and have an even thickness. Craft felt is less expensive and also comes in lots of colors. Craft felt isn't as high quality as wool felt and may have an uneven thickness (thinner or thicker areas on the same piece of felt).

Stuffing

Use polyester, cotton, or wool stuffing for fairy projects. One bag makes many, many fairy crafts!

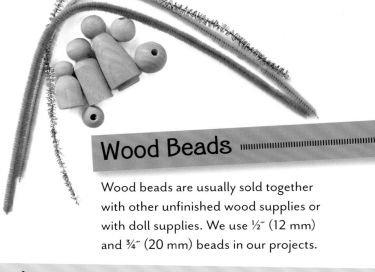

Chenille Stems

Also called *pipe cleaners*, chenille stems come in many colors and may even be sparkly. We use 12˝-long pipe cleaners for our fairy bodies. We snip them shorter when making baby fairies.

Wood Beads

Wood beads are usually sold together with other unfinished wood supplies or with doll supplies. We use ½˝ (12 mm) and ¾˝ (20 mm) beads in our projects.

Peg People

Wooden peg people are the base for gnomes, and they are sold together with other unfinished wood supplies. We use 1¹¹⁄₁₆˝ peg people. If you use a different size, you might need to modify the size of the gnome patterns to fit your peg person.

Flower Petals

Fabric flowers make excellent dresses and wings for fairies. Also called *silk flowers* and *faux flowers*, fabric flowers are sold in craft stores and online. Occasionally, you can find a collection of loose petals with scrapbook supplies.

You can take apart flowers to use the petals. Look for medium-size flowers when making a petal dress. If the petals are too tiny, they will tear when trying to make a skirt. Tiny blossoms can be perfect for decorating hats or baby fairies, however.

Look closely at the stem when buying flowers for their petals. If the flower is *not* held together with gobs of glue, it will work for fairies! At home, pull the flower off the stem and separate the petals. Flowers change with the seasons at craft stores; mix and match the colors to celebrate the year.

Gerbera daisies make great skirts and tiger lily petals make perfect wings. Petals that have a thin strip of plastic to hold their shape are ideal for wings because they will stay upright on a fairy's back. Clip a pair of wings from the rest of the petals.

Decorations

Decorations are everywhere! Use sequins, beads, buttons, and little jingle bells to add glitz to your fairies. Buttons can become eyes on animal crafts, and pretty ribbons are wonderful decorations that you can sew onto crafts. Wire-edged ribbon makes great wings because you can bend it into curvy shapes. Store decorations in little bowls, jars, or small bags (which are sold in the beading section of craft stores).

Acorn Caps

Look to nature for inspiration. For example, acorn caps (the top parts of acorns) make great fairy hats. If you live near oak trees, look beneath your feet in the fall and collect acorn caps that have fallen to the ground. If a cap is still stuck on an acorn, let the acorn dry in your home for a few days. Then wiggle the cap right off.

Every acorn cap is unique. We fill our pockets when we see acorns scattered below an oak tree. To make an acorn cap into a hat, test it on your fairy to see whether it fits and looks good. Add a dab of glue to keep it in place. If you live in an area without oak trees, ask a friend to send you some acorn caps, or purchase them online from A Child's Dream (achildsdream.com).

Fairy Crafting Supply Checklist

Many of these items can be found at home. In the case that you need to go to the store, here's a handy list to bring along. You won't need every item for each project, so get started with what you have!

Crafting Supplies

- ⬡ ¾˝ and ½˝ wood beads
- ⬡ Chenille stems (pipe cleaners)
- ⬡ Craft glue (such as Aleene's Tacky Glue)
- ⬡ Dry beans for beanbags

- ⬡ Needles
- ⬡ Peg people size 1¹¹⁄₁₆˝ for gnomes
- ⬡ Stuffing
- ⬡ Thread

Fabrics

- ⬡ Felt (felt wool, wool blend, or craft felt)

Decorations

- ⬡ Acorn caps
- ⬡ Beads
- ⬡ Bells
- ⬡ Buttons
- ⬡ Fancy sequins or buttons (like snowflakes)

- ⬡ Miniature pom-poms
- ⬡ Sequins
- ⬡ Silk flowers
- ⬡ Wire-edged ribbon
- ⬡ Yarn

Tools

- ⬡ Scissors

Optional

- ⬡ Aromatic dry herbs like lavender, tea bags, or cinnamon sticks
- ⬡ Floral wire for the wedding arch
- ⬡ Miniature wire flowers for fairy bouquets
- ⬡ Pinking shears

- ⬡ Ribbon
- ⬡ Rotary cutter with wavy or scalloped blade
- ⬡ Safety pins
- ⬡ Wood circles for the wedding arch

Sewing Lessons

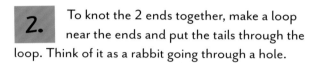

STITCHING WORKSHOP

1. Pass your thread through the eye of a needle: Hold the needle steady with one hand while you thread the eye with the other hand. (Sometimes it helps to lick the thread first.) Pull the thread gently until both ends are even.

Starting Knot

2. To knot the 2 ends together, make a loop near the ends and put the tails through the loop. Think of it as a rabbit going through a hole.

3. Tug on the ends until the knot is tight. Do not cut the ends too close to the knot—it may come undone!

1. Take a little stitch on the back of the felt to hide the knot. Push the needle down into the felt near the edge.

2. Move the needle a little way along the edge of the felt from the first stitch. Push the needle back through the felt to the bottom.

POLAR BEAR Whipstitch

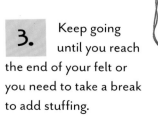

3. Keep going until you reach the end of your felt or you need to take a break to add stuffing.

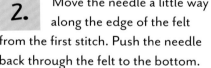

Imagine your needle is a polar bear and your felt is an iceberg. The polar bear wants to jump on the ice, but he's heavy and falls through. Now he's back in the ocean! Keep him jumping through the felt iceberg all the way around the edge.

1. Start at the back of the felt to hide the knot, and push the needle to the top. Push the needle down through the felt from above. Pull the thread, but not so tight that the felt wrinkles. Now your first stitch shows.

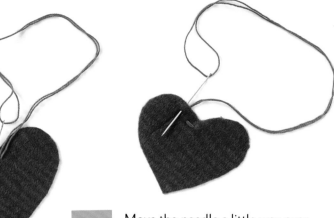

DOLPHIN
Running Stitch

Imagine that your needle is a dolphin. Your dolphin jumps up out of the water and then back down into the water. Dolphins love jumping!

2. Move the needle a little way over and push it up from below the felt. Pull the needle gently until the thread comes up to the top.

3. Keep going!

SEED STITCH

The seed stitch is lots of little dolphin running stitches. Make tiny stitches going up and down, up and down, all over your felt. These stitches can look like raindrops, blades of grass, or little seeds (like the ones on strawberries!).

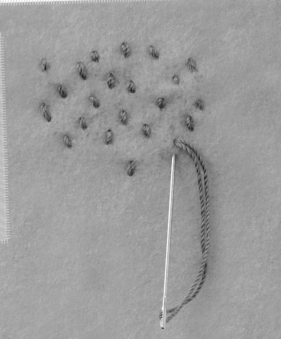

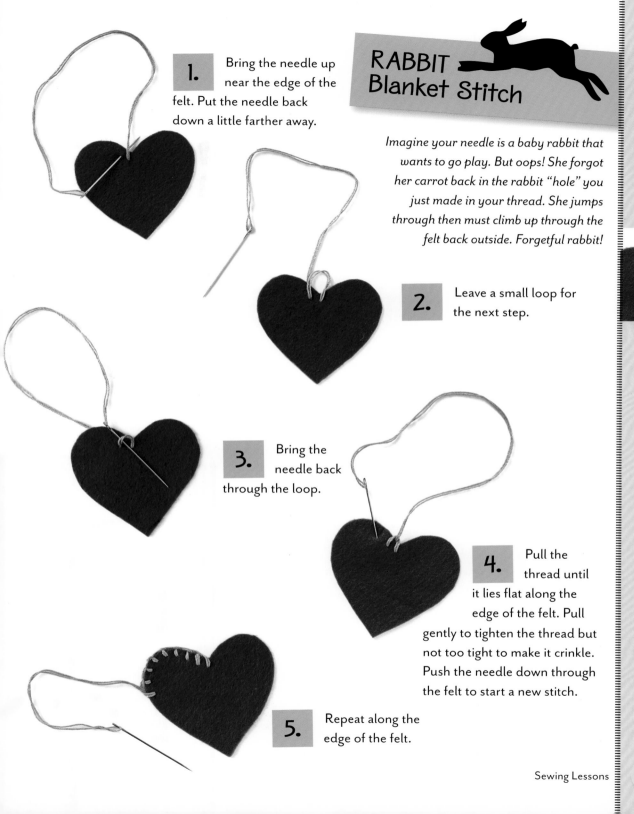

1. Bring the needle up near the edge of the felt. Put the needle back down a little farther away.

RABBIT Blanket Stitch

Imagine your needle is a baby rabbit that wants to go play. But oops! She forgot her carrot back in the rabbit "hole" you just made in your thread. She jumps through then must climb up through the felt back outside. Forgetful rabbit!

2. Leave a small loop for the next step.

3. Bring the needle back through the loop.

4. Pull the thread until it lies flat along the edge of the felt. Pull gently to tighten the thread but not too tight to make it crinkle. Push the needle down through the felt to start a new stitch.

5. Repeat along the edge of the felt.

MANTA RAY
Backstitch

Have you ever seen manta rays feeding on plankton? They swim along the ocean floor doing backflips in the water to scoop plankton into their mouths. Imagine that your needle is a manta ray doing backflips along the felt.

1. Start by sewing a single stitch: Pull the needle up and then push it down, like a dolphin running stitch (page 14).

2. Push the needle up through the felt a little distance from the end of the first stitch. It will look like you're leaving a gap between stitches, but don't sew forward. Instead, push the needle *backwards* into the felt—toward the first stitch so it looks like one long stitch.

3. Continue going forward and back, and you will create a continuous line of thread. This stitch is perfect for decorating stems and leaves.

Finishing Knot

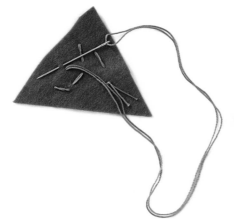

1. After sewing on decorations, finish by tying a quick knot. Just dip the needle into the felt near the last stitch. Do this on the back of the project if you can.

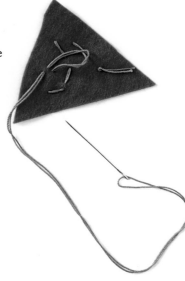

2. Pull the needle through until you have a little loop. Push the needle through that loop.

3. Pull the thread tight.

4. Repeat Steps 2 and 3 a couple of times to be sure that your knot will hold. Don't cut the thread too close to the knot or it will come undone. Leave a little tail.

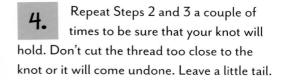

SIMPLE FINISHING KNOT

Tie together two thread ends on the back of the project. To do this, snip the needle off of the thread and use the two tails to tie a knot just like you would on your shoes. Do this twice and you will have a good, strong knot.

SEWING LESSONS
STITCHING WORKSHOP

1. To tie a knot, make one end of the thread go under the other end of your thread.

DOUBLE KNOT

2. Pull both ends to make a knot, just like tying your shoes.

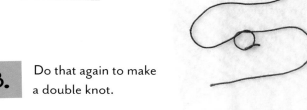

3. Do that again to make a double knot.

DOUBLE BOW

1. To make a bow, pinch one side of your thread together like a rabbit ear. Pinch the other thread to make another rabbit ear.

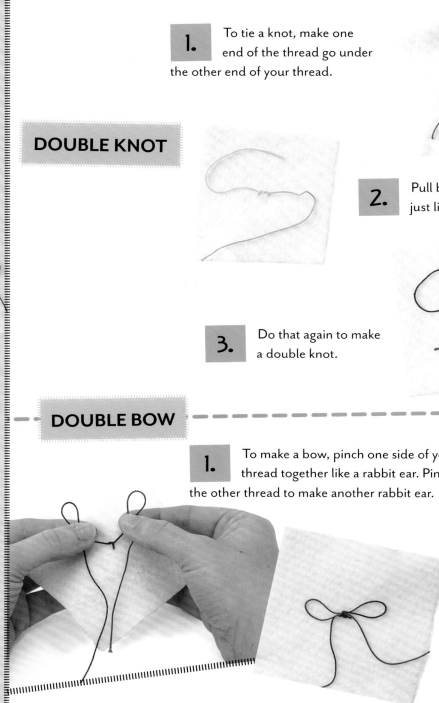

2. Make one rabbit ear tie a knot with the other ear. Go under; then gently tug on both loops to make a bow.

3. Tie them in another knot to make a double bow.

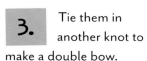

1. Trace the pattern outline onto a piece of paper. Cut out the shape on the line to make a pattern piece.

Using Patterns

Here's how you use the patterns at the back of the book to cut shapes from felt.

2. Place the pattern piece on your felt and pin it in place with a safety pin. Trace onto the felt with a pencil or pen, marking carefully around the shape.

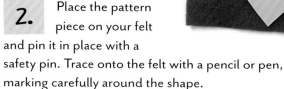

3. Unpin the paper and cut out the shape from the felt. It may be easiest to cut out all of the shapes that you need before starting to sew. Keep the pieces together in a basket or bag.

TIP

Be sure you have enough felt for a project by placing the pattern pieces on the felt before cutting. Check to see if you need more than one of a particular shape. Place patterns smartly—near the edge and close together—so you will be able to get more fairy pieces out of your felt.

CUTTING ON THE FOLD

Some pattern pieces direct you to cut out a shape from a piece of felt that is folded in half.

1. Be sure to start with felt that is twice as big as your pattern. Fold the felt in half, and place the pattern on the folded edge.

2. Pin the pattern in place with a safety pin. Cut out around the shape through both layers of felt. Do *not* cut along the folded edge of the felt.

3. Remove the pin. Open the felt to reveal a perfect shape. Well done!

Sewing Lessons

Adding Decorations

Make your crafts special by sewing on sequins, beads, and buttons.

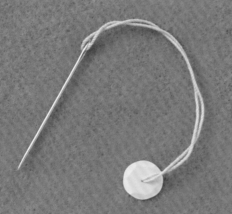

SEQUINS AND BEADS

Decide where you want to place a sequin or bead. Start in the back of the felt and push the needle up at that spot. Push the needle through the hole in the sequin or bead; then slide it down onto the felt. Push the needle back down through the felt to the side of the sequin or bead. Decide where the next decoration belongs and repeat the sewing steps. Tie a knot after the last one. Be careful to only add sequins or beads to the side of the felt that will show.

CREATIVE IDEA

You can add a bead to the center of sequins with a neat little trick. Sew up through a sequin, and push the sequin down along the thread until it's resting on the felt. Push your needle through a bead and then back through the center of the sequin and through the felt. You don't need to stitch around the outside of your sequin—the bead will hold your sequin in place.

BUTTONS

Buttons with two holes are the easiest to sew, but you can also use buttons with four holes.

Push your needle up where you want the button to be. Slide the button down to the felt; then push the needle back down the button's hole and through the felt. You may want to repeat the steps a few times to give your button a strong hold on the felt.

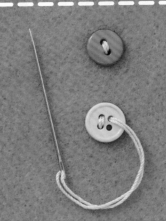

Fairies and gnomes find many ways to express themselves. One way is with decorative edges along hatbands, shirts, and capes. You can choose different ways to make your fairy clothes fancy. Start with ruffles, points, and waves, and then see if you create new kinds of edges.

Fancy Edges

RUFFLES

To make edges ruffle, snip a little ways into the felt from the edge. Ruffles can be long or short. Just be careful not to clip them too close together or the felt can fall into pieces.

PINKING SHEARS

Pinking shears can make fun ruffles. Pinking shears are scissors with zigzag-shaped blades that are made for fabric. Cut along one edge of the felt with the pinking shears. Then clip a little bit between each zigzag to make a ruffle. This technique makes wonderful petal designs, too, especially at the bottom of a fairy shirt.

POINTS

For pointy shapes, cut away small triangles along an edge of the felt. Start from the outside edge and cut a short diagonal line into the felt. Move the felt a bit and cut another diagonal to meet the first cut. You just cut a triangle!

CUTTING TIP

Cut away each triangle instead of trying to go "around" the triangle shapes.

Continue along until the edge of your felt looks pointy. Points cut into a hatband look like a crown. This technique also works for making petals. Make your cuts slightly curvy to look like petal shapes.

You can also use this technique with a circle to make a little flower shape or a sun!

WAVES

Add waves along your felt. Start cutting at one end of the felt and aim the scissors a little back and forth slowly as you go. If you draw a wavy line with a marker before cutting, you will have a path to follow.

ROTARY CUTTER

A rotary cutter with a scalloped edge can makes nice curvy edges. A rotary cutter is a round cutting tool that has circular blades. It looks a lot like a pizza cutter, but it is made for fabric. Ask an adult to help anytime you use a rotary cutter. They are super sharp and they roll fast.

All crafters make mistakes, even grown-ups! If you have a problem when you're sewing, remember two important things: Stay calm, and don't pull the needle too tight! Here are great ways to fix common problems.

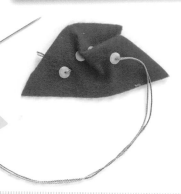

SAFETY NOTE
Never give toys with wood beads, buttons, or sequins to a baby or toddler.

TANGLED THREAD

Tangling can happen when thread twists or is very long. You can also get tangles if you don't pull the thread all the way before starting your next stitch. Gently tug on knots until they loosen, and ask an adult if you need help. Or try using a shorter piece of thread. Crochet thread size 10 helps avoid tangles.

SCRUNCHING

If you pull your stitches too tight, the whole project can squish up into a mess. Be patient! This problem can be solved with a little loosening. Tug at one stitch at a time until you can flatten the felt. Ask an adult if you feel overwhelmed. Practice making stitches that are not too loose or too tight—stitches that are just right.

Here's a simple trick: If you worry about decorations coming loose, secure them as you sew. Tie a little knot on the back after adding a sequin. The knot keeps the sequin from coming loose. Then go where you want to add the next sequin. Do this extra step if you want to play with the toy a lot or give the craft to a child four to six years old (they like to pull on things).

LOOSE BUTTONS, BEADS, OR SEQUINS

Sometimes a sewn decoration can become loose. Either a little friend pulls on the sequin, or the threads get loose. If you are lucky and it's not glued, you can tug it back into place from the back side of the felt.

If that doesn't work, clip the loose threads. Tie two knots over the decoration.

basic fairy family

*These first fairies are a great place to start crafting forest friends.
All the other fairies in the book start out like these simpler ones,
so you will be turning back to these directions again and again.
To make it easy to find the instructions you need later,
some of the pages are labeled on the sides.*

*You will learn to make a fairy family that includes a girl, a boy, a
baby, and a gnome. Make them your own by adding special details!*

*Before you begin, learn about felt, needles, and other necessary
supplies by turning to Things You Will Need (page 9). Visit Sewing
Lessons (page 13) to learn about stitching and other skills.*

fairy girl

FINISHED FAIRY:
About 5˝ high with hat

simple

Choose your favorite colors depending on the season. You can start with this fairy and learn the skills you will need to make more fairy friends.

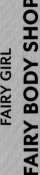

Making Your Fairy

Fairy Body Shop

- -

Making a fairy body can be tricky, especially at first. Take it a step at a time. If you want to adjust the length of the arms or legs, just unbend the chenille and bend it again.

- -

You Will Need

Before you start, see if you have felt pieces big enough for the patterns you need to cut out. For this project you will use the Fairy dress, hat, and hatband patterns (pages 132 and 133). Makes 1 fairy.

- **1 piece of felt** for hat
- **1 piece of felt** for hatband
- **1 piece of felt** for dress
- **¾″ wood bead** for head
- **2 chenille stems** 12″ long for body
- **Yarn** for hair
- **Wired ribbon** 4″ long for wings
- **Sequins and beads**
- **Thread**
- **Small amount of stuffing** for body and hat
- **Craft glue** (such as Aleene's Original Tacky Glue)
- **1 tiny bell** for hat (*if you want*)

1. Choose a chenille stem for the fairy's legs. Fold the stem in half.

2. About 2″ from the top bend, fold the long ends again. Make a W shape with really long ends.

3. Choose another chenille stem for the fairy's arms. Fold it in half and slip it in the middle of the W.

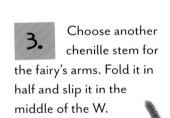

Fairy Girl   27

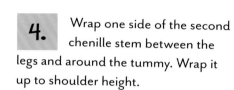

4. Wrap one side of the second chenille stem between the legs and around the tummy. Wrap it up to shoulder height.

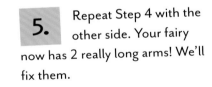

5. Repeat Step 4 with the other side. Your fairy now has 2 really long arms! We'll fix them.

6. Bend the long arms back toward the fairy's tummy. Tuck the loose ends into the fairy's tummy. Try not to let wire poke out.

Faces Workshop

- -

Choose any kind of face for your fairy. Draw, paint, or leave the bead blank and imagine any expression you want—happy or sad, excited or sleepy. Blank faces are lovely.

- -

TIP

To make fairies with various skin tones, paint the beads with watercolors. Use brown tones or bright colors—fairies can be any color of the rainbow! Always wait for the paint to dry before drawing on beads.

Colored Pencils

The quickest way to draw a face on beads is with colored pencils. You can do this directly on the wooden bead.

Markers

To use pens to draw faces, cover the beads with a thin layer of Liquitex Matte Varnish or Mod Podge first. If you don't, the marker will seep or bleed into the wood grain and the fairy may appear to be crying. Liquid varnish can be found near acrylic paints in craft stores.

It's tricky to brush varnish on a small round bead when it's in your hands. Instead, fold a chenille stem in half and slip a bead (or several) on it. Now you can brush on varnish without getting your fingers sticky! Prop the stem on top of a glass while the beads dry.

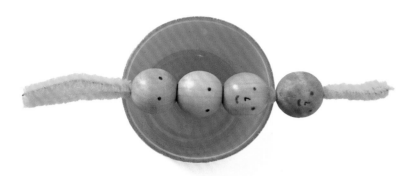

Use regular-tip permanent markers for the eyes and mouth. Use a fine-point (thin) marker for the nose.

Making Faces

The expression on a face can convey many different moods. Practice on a piece of paper by drawing circles and trying out different ideas. We included some fairy favorites to inspire you.

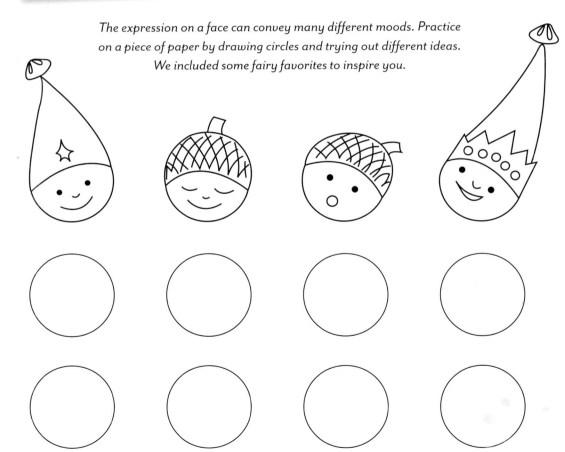

Dress Shop

Fairies dress up at the local dress shop. They love all of the colors and fancy threads.

1. Cut out felt using the Fairy dress pattern (page 132).

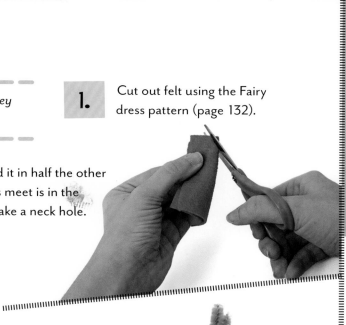

2. Fold the dress in half; then fold it in half the other way. The place where the folds meet is in the center. Cut across that little corner to make a neck hole.

3. Slide the dress over the fairy's neck.

CREATIVE IDEA

Fairies of all sizes are welcome in the forest! Give yours more substance by wrapping a bit of stuffing around its waist before adding a dress. Wool stuffing works best, but any type of stuffing can be used.

4. Cut a long piece of thread about twice as long as your arm. Lay the thread on a table. Place the fairy facedown on top of the thread so that one tail of the thread is extra long and the other is about 6˝ long.

5. Tie a tight knot under the fairy's arms. The tight knot will gather the fairy's dress at the waist. You may want to ask an adult to help you tie a very tight knot.

Fairy Girl

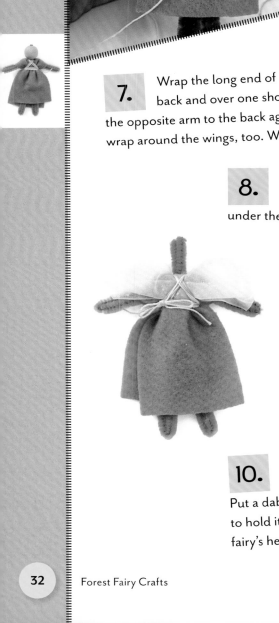

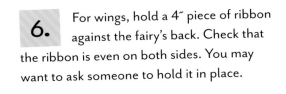

6. For wings, hold a 4″ piece of ribbon against the fairy's back. Check that the ribbon is even on both sides. You may want to ask someone to hold it in place.

7. Wrap the long end of the thread from the back and over one shoulder. Bring it under the opposite arm to the back again. The thread will wrap around the wings, too. Wrap it 2 more times.

8. Switch sides. Go over the other shoulder and under the other arm 3 times.

9. Keep going around the waist, over the shoulders, and under the arms. Wrap until the thread is almost used up. Tie the ends together in the back with a double knot (page 18) and tie a bow. Double knot (page 18) the bow so it doesn't come untied.

10. Spread out the wings and shape them however you like. Put a dab of glue inside the wood bead to hold it on the chenille stem. Slide the fairy's head onto the neck. Lovely!

Hair Studio

Fairies get fancy with their hairstyles. Use any color that inspires you. Create short and wild hair, long and loose hair, or fancy braided hair.

The first step is choosing yarn. You don't need very much.

Any soft yarn will work nicely for fairy hair. One of our favorites is called *eyelash yarn*; this yarn is fluffy with lots of little "eyelashes." For braids, we prefer cotton yarns because they don't unravel at the ends. You can even combine yarns to get unique looks.

Play around with the yarn to see which style you like. We included three of our favorite styles. You will need craft glue to hold the hair on your fairy's head.

To start, find a small container to hold your fairy. Bend her arms over the edge so she balances on the edge of the container. Go to the style that you like for the next directions.

CREATIVE IDEA

You can use hair and skip making a hat for your fairy. Layer the yarn until the wood bead is covered.

Fancy-Free

This is the fastest way to give a fairy hair. It's perfect for fairies who would rather fly around than fuss with long hair.

1. Wrap yarn around your fingers about 6 times. Spread your fingers apart for longer hair or closer together for shorter hair. Clip the end of the yarn.

2. Place a dab of glue on the top of the fairy's head. Pinch the wrapped yarn in the middle; hold that together and place it gently on the glue on your fairy's head. You can arrange the yarn so it lies flatter and each strand is touching the glue. Leave the yarn in loops so it doesn't unravel.

3. When you are happy with how the yarn looks, let the glue dry. Now your fairy is ready for a hat! Go to the hat shop (page 36).

Long and Loose

Long hair needs yarn that doesn't fall apart when the ends are cut. Use yarn that won't unravel or leave the yarn in loops instead of snipping the ends. Tie little strings around the yarn to make ponytails.

1. Place a piece of yarn over the fairy's head so it hangs down on either side. It needs to go over both sides of the head. Cut a few more strands the same length—the number depends on the thickness of your yarn and the look you want.

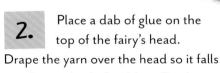

2. Place a dab of glue on the top of the fairy's head. Drape the yarn over the head so it falls evenly over both shoulders. Do the same with the other strands. Let the glue dry. If you want a hat, go to the hat shop (page 36).

Fancy Braids

*Our braids use multicolored cotton yarn for a fun effect.
You can also mix yarns to create dramatic braids.*

1. Run a piece of yarn from the fairy's foot, over the head, and back to the other foot. Cut it off. Measure 5 more pieces the same length so you have 6 in all.

TIP
You need to have a fairy hat ready to go before the next step. Head over to the hat shop (page 36) and make one. Then come back here and continue to make fancy braids.

2. Add a dab of glue to the top of the head. Place the 6 strands of yarn on the top of the fairy's head. Line up the yarn over the glue so the strands lie flat. Glue the fairy's hat (page 36) over her hair before making the braids. Let all of the glue dry completely before braiding the yarn.

Fairy shown
from the back

3. When all the glue has dried, it's time to braid. Each braid has 6 threads; divide them into 3 groups of 2 threads. Braid the yarn to make short or longer braids. Ask an adult to help if you want. Tie the braid with a piece of thread that you double knot, and clip any uneven pieces of yarn at the end of the braids.

Have fun thinking of many other creative ways to style fairy hair!

Hat Shop

- -

Be creative when decorating a fairy's hat. Think of the colors outside and make a hat that celebrates the season.

- -

1. Cut out felt using the Fairy hat and hatband patterns (page 133). Check the fit by wrapping the hat around the fairy's head to be sure you like the size. Choose beads and sequins to decorate the hat. Collect them in a small bowl to keep them from rolling away.

2. Thread a needle and knot the thread. Hold the hatband on the felt, using a safety pin if you want to hold it in place. Start the needle from the back of the hat so the knot will be hidden. Sew the decorations onto the front of the hat. Be sure that a few decorations are on the hatband to hold that in place. See Sequins and Beads (page 20) for help. Make sure to sew all the sequins to the outside of the hat! When you are finished with decorating, take off the safety pin if you used one.

3. Fold the hat in half so the 2 sides match. Sew the felt together at the bottom of the hat with a couple stitches.

4. Keep sewing up the back of the hat using the polar bear whipstitch (page 13) or the rabbit blanket stitch (page 15). If you like, sew more sequins and beads on the edge of the hat as you go along.

5. If you want, string a bell onto the thread to add it to top of the hat. Tie a finishing knot (page 17) at the top. To hide the extra thread, push the needle to the inside of the hat. Pull a little on the thread and then snip it. When you straighten the felt, the end will disappear into the hat.

6. Put a tiny bit of stuffing inside the hat. Put a dab of glue on the top front and top back of the fairy's head. This will keep the hat secure. Be careful not to use too much glue because it can drip or soak the felt. An adult can help with the glue at first.

TIP: ADD FLAIR

Make a hat that's extra fancy by following the instructions for adding a bell and beads (below).

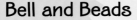

Bell and Beads

For more sparkle, add extra beads and a bell to the top of a hat.

1. After sewing up a hat, thread the needle through extra beads and a bell.

2. Push the needle back down through the beads and into the hat. Now the bell will hang at the end of the beads.

3. Pull the thread tight and tie a knot.

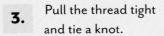

Fairy Girl

fairy boy

FINISHED FAIRY:
About 5˝ high with hat

simple

This fairy is wearing pants and a shirt. Use these instructions when making other fairies in the book who are wearing the same clothes. We call this a "fairy boy" to keep our directions simple. But, of course, girl fairies can wear pants and boy fairies may wear dresses. The magic of the forest is that you get to choose!

You Will Need

Before you start, see if you have felt pieces big enough for the patterns you need to cut out. For this project you will use the Fairy shirt, pants, hat, and hatband patterns (pages 132 and 133). Makes 1 fairy.

- **1 piece of felt** for hat
- **1 piece of felt** for hatband
- **1 piece of felt** for shirt
- **1 piece of felt** for pants
- **¾˝ wood bead** for head
- **2 chenille stems** 12˝ long for body
- **Wired ribbon** 4˝ long for wings
- **Sequins and little beads**
- **Thread**
- **Small amount of stuffing** for hat
- **Craft glue** (such as Aleene's Original Tacky Glue)
- **1 tiny bell** for hat (if you want)

Making Your Fairy

Make a fairy body following the directions in Fairy Body Shop (page 27). For the face, visit the faces workshop (page 29). Learn how to make a hat in the hat shop (page 36). When you are ready for the clothes, come back here!

Pants and Shirt Shop

At first, the pants start out like a fairy dress. But wait and see— you will magically turn the felt piece into pants.

1. Cut out felt using the Fairy pants and shirt patterns (page 132).

2. Start with the pants. Fold the felt piece in half; then fold it in half the other way. The place where the folds meet is the center. Cut across that little corner to make a neck hole.

3. Slide the pants over the fairy's neck. Cut the felt in the middle, between the legs. Cut a slit up both the front and the back. This will make the pant legs.

4. Cut a long piece of thread about twice as long as your arm. Lay the thread on a table. Place the fairy facedown on top of the thread so that one tail of the thread is extra long and the other is about 6˝ long. Tie a tight knot in the back under your fairy's arms to gather the pants at the waist.

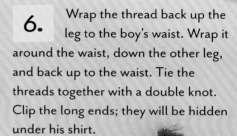

5. Wrap the longest thread around one leg so the felt wraps around the leg. When you do this for the first time, you may want an adult to help you.

6. Wrap the thread back up the leg to the boy's waist. Wrap it around the waist, down the other leg, and back up to the waist. Tie the threads together with a double knot. Clip the long ends; they will be hidden under his shirt.

7. It's time to make the shirt! Fold the shirt piece in half twice as you did with the pants in Step 1. Clip the corner to create a neck hole for the shirt. Slide the shirt over the fairy's neck.

CREATIVE IDEA

Cut special patterns along the hem of the shirt. Try a zigzag or fringe. See Fancy Edges (page 21).

8. Cut a long piece of thread about twice as long as your arm. Tie it tight under the fairy's arms as you did in Step 4. Pick up the 4˝ piece of ribbon for the wings. Hold the ribbon against the fairy's back. Make sure the ribbon is even on both sides.

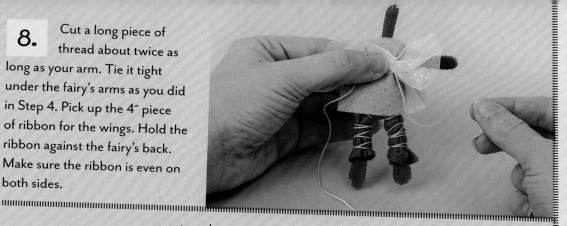

9. Wrap the long end of the thread from the back and over one shoulder. Bring it under the opposite arm to the back again. Wrap it twice. The thread will wrap around the wings, too.

10. Go over the other shoulder and under the other arm. Keep going around the waist, over the shoulders, and under the arms. Wrap until the thread is almost gone. Tie the threads together and make a bow. Double knot the bow (page 18) so it stays secure.

11. Spread out the wings and shape them however you like. Put a dab of glue inside the wood bead for the head. Slide the head onto his neck. Hurrah! Your fairy has clothes.

Finishing Your Fairy

1. Often, boy fairies don't have hair. But if you want to add some, follow the directions for the style that you like in the hair studio (page 33).

2. Cut out felt using the Fairy hat and hatband patterns (page 133). Then make a hat following the directions in Hat Shop (page 36). Use a dab of glue to hold the hat on the fairy's head and let it dry.

Go have fun together!

Fairy Boy

fairy baby

FINISHED FAIRY:
About 1˝

fancy

Fairy babies are adorable. Even though they are tiny, they love to dress up in seasonal colors!

You Will Need

Before you start, see if you have felt pieces big enough for the patterns you need to cut out. For this project you will use the Fairy Baby body and hat patterns (page 133). Makes 1 fairy baby.

- **1 piece of felt** for body
- **½˜ wood bead** for head
- **1 chenille stem** clipped to 6˜ long for body frame
- **Sequins, buttons, and/or small silk flowers**
- **Acorn cap or scrap of felt** for hat
- **Thread**
- **Stuffing** for body
- **Craft glue** (such as Aleene's Original Tacky Glue)
- **1 tiny bell** for felt hat (*if you want*)
- **Small pair of silk flowers** for wings (*if you want*)

Making Your Fairy Baby Face and Body

1. Cut out felt using the Fairy Baby body pattern (page 133).

2. On the wood bead, draw a sweet face or leave the bead plain. For help, visit the faces workshop (page 29).

3. The little fairy has a chenille-stem frame that goes inside the felt body. To make the frame, fold a chenille stem in half and put the wood bead over the folded end. Leave a little of the fold sticking out of the top of the bead. Bend the folded stem back against the bead.

4. Open the 2 chenille stem ends so they stick out sideways from the bead. Fold each of these ends in half to make the arms.

5. Fold the fairy baby body in half at the shoulders, then in half again. Clip the corner to make a little neck hole.

6. Sew a decoration onto the front of the baby's body. A sequin, button, or tiny flower petal looks adorable.

7. On the chenille stem body frame, straighten the top of the stem and take off the bead. Put the stem through the hole in the felt body so the wire arms are under the felt. Put a tiny dab of glue inside the head. Put the head back on, and re-bend the folded chenille stem against the bead.

8. Fold the felt body in half at the shoulders, making sure the decoration is on the outside. Pin the sides together with a safety pin to keep it steady. Sew around the edges of the body using either a polar bear whipstitch (page 13) or the rabbit blanket stitch (page 15). Stop sewing when you are most of the way around to leave a small opening. Take off the safety pin. Put in the stuffing. When the fairy baby is nice and puffy, sew the opening shut.

9. If you want tiny, tiny wings, sew little flower petals or a scrap of ribbon on the back with a couple of stitches.

10. Glue an acorn cap to the fairy's head, or sew a small hat from a triangle of felt following the directions in Hat Shop (page 36).

Your fairy baby is ready to join the celebration!

gnome

simple

FINISHED GNOME:
About 2½˝

Gnomes are good little friends to the fairies. They welcome each new season with festive colors and decorations, and they are perfect for using up little scraps of felt. Finished gnomes add to seasonal tables, shelves, and games.

You Will Need

We use size 1 ¹¹/₁₆˝ peg people for our gnomes. If you have a different size, check the project pattern pieces to be sure the felt pieces will fit. Before you start, see if you have felt pieces big enough for the patterns you need to cut out. For this project you will use the Gnome body, cape, hat, and hatband patterns (page 133). Makes 1 gnome.

- **1 piece of felt** for hat
- **1 piece of felt** for hatband
- **1 piece of felt** for cape
- **1 piece of felt** for body
- **1 wood peg person** size 1¹¹/₁₆˝
- **Sequins and/or beads** for hat
- **1 tiny bell** for hat
- **Thread**
- **Tiny amount of stuffing** for hat
- **Craft glue** (such as Aleene's Original Tacky Glue)
- **Thin yarn** for hair (*if you want*)

Making Your Gnome

1. Cut out felt using the Gnome body, cape, hat, and hatband patterns (page 133).

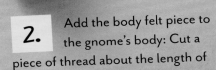

2. Add the body felt piece to the gnome's body: Cut a piece of thread about the length of your arm. Hold the piece of felt around the gnome's tummy, and tie the thread around the gnome with one tail longer than the other. This will hold the felt in place. Position the knot in the back, leaving one tail long and the other short.

TIP
We like to tie felt onto the gnome with thread, but you can glue a strip of fabric around the gnome's tummy. Use a hair-tie or rubber band to hold the felt in place while it dries. Use the glue sparingly or it will soak through the felt.

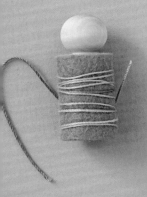

3. Wrap the thread around and around the gnome. This will decorate the gnome and hold the felt in place. Fancy! The thread might get loose around the neck, but adding the cape later will cover it up, so don't worry about that part of the gnome. When you feel done, tie the threads with 2 knots in the back and clip any long pieces. The knot will be hidden under the cape.

TIP: DON'T CUT TOO CLOSE!
Be careful not to trim too close to a knot, or it might come undone.

4. Place the cape around the gnome's neck to see if you like how it fits. Cut it smaller if it is too big.

Sew the cape onto the gnome. If you want to hide the knot, start sewing at the back of the cape. Sew to the front with a couple of dolphin running stitches (page 14).

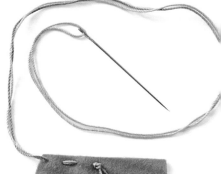

CREATIVE IDEA

Add sequins or beads to the outside of the cape. Or layer two colors of felt and sew around the outside edges to hold them together. You can also make two layers of capes that are shaped differently; they could look like petals or water. Gnomes love creative capes!

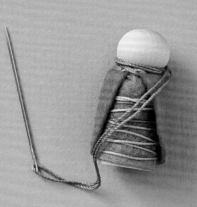

5. Sew the cape together with 1 or 2 stitches (2 if you want it stronger).

6. Wrap the thread around the neck a few times. Tie a knot at the back if you want to hide the knot under the hat.

7. If you like, glue a little hair on the gnome. You can use thin yarn and make braids. For directions, see Hair Studio (page 33). Leave the face plain or draw 2 little dots for eyes with colored pencils. To learn how to color and draw on wood with watercolors, pencils, or markers, see Faces Workshop (page 29).

8. Cut out a gnome hat and hatband. Sew on decorations as described in Hat Shop (page 36). Be careful not to add too many decorations—the hat could get heavy and make your gnome topple over! Fold the hat in half, and sew up the back. Tie a knot and clip the extra thread. Add a pinch of stuffing inside the hat, and glue the hat on your gnome.

spring

Spring is when flowers wake up and dance in the breeze. So do the spring fairies! The fairies can be any color that you see in the garden or in nature. Choose color combinations that say "spring" to you!

Fairies dress up with lots and lots of petals in springtime. You can use petals for many different fairies.

simple spring fairies and gnome

FINISHED FAIRY:
About 5˝ high with hat

FINISHED GNOME: 3˝

You Will Need

To make 1 fairy, use the supplies listed under What Every Fairy Needs and either Fairy Girl or Fairy Boy.

WHAT EVERY FAIRY NEEDS

- **¾˝ wood bead** for head
- **2 chenille stems** 12˝ long for body
- **1 pair of silk flowers or leaves** for wings
- **Sequins and beads**
- **1 tiny bell** for hat
- **Thread**
- **A pinch of stuffing**
- **Craft glue** (such as Aleene's Original Tacky Glue)

FAIRY GIRL

- **1 piece of felt** for hat
- **1 piece of felt** for hatband
- **1 piece of felt** for shirt
- **Silk flower petals** for skirt
- **Yarn** for hair
- **Tiny silk flower petals** to decorate hat

FAIRY BOY

- **1 piece of felt** for hat
- **2 pieces of felt** for decorating hat
- **1 piece of felt** for shirt
- **1 piece of felt** for pants

Making Your Spring Fairy Girl

Before you start, see if you have felt pieces big enough for the patterns you need to cut out. For this project you will use the Fairy shirt, hat, and hatband patterns (pages 132 and 133).

Face and Body

Make the fairy's body and face. Use one chenille stem for the legs and another for the arms. For help, see Faces Workshop (page 29) and Fairy Body Shop (page 27).

CREATIVE IDEA

Boy and girl fairies both love wearing pants in the springtime. Choose whatever outfit makes you and your fairy happy!

Tiger lily petals make beautiful wings.

Spring Petal Dress Top and Wings

1. Cut out felt using the Fairy shirt pattern (page 132). The shirt will become the top of the fairy's dress. We will use petals for her skirt, which you will add later.

2. Take apart the flower that you are using for the wings. Cut the ring of petals so that 2 petals are attached in the middle. These will be the fairy's wings. Be careful not to cut them apart.

PETAL TIP

The flower petals that you use for the wings don't need to be the same as the flowers that you use for the fairy's skirt. Look for flowers that have a nice shape for wings, or use silk leaves. For help, see Things You Will Need, Flower Petals (page 10).

3. Put the felt shirt on the fairy the same way you did the dress for Fairy Girl. For details, visit the dress shop (page 31). Wrap thread around the shirt and the petal wings. Tie off the thread with a double-knotted bow (page 18). Now your fairy can fly!

CREATIVE IDEA

If you have pinking shears, you could use them on the hem of the shirt to make a zigzag pattern. Clip between the points to make ruffles. To learn how to make ruffles and other edge decorations, see Fancy Edges (page 21).

Flower Petal Skirt

Learn more about flower petals in Things You Will Need, Flower Petals (page 10).

1. Choose 3–6 petals in different sizes. Put them in a pile, with the biggest petal on the bottom and the smallest on the top. Try different combinations until you the find one that you like best. You are the dress designer!

2. With scissors, clip a *teeny-tiny* line out from the center of the petal. The fairy's feet will go through this hole. Do not cut too far, or the petals will tear and the skirt will fall off!

3. Gently put the fairy's feet through the hole in the smallest flower petal first. This will be the top of her skirt. Scoot the petal up gently to the fairy's waist; then add the next petal and the next.

4. Add all of the other petals, one at a time. Work from the smallest to the biggest and fluff out the petals. Admire the lovely dress!

5. Put a dab of glue inside the bead head. Place the head on the body.

Hat

1. Cut out felt using the Fairy hat and hatband patterns (page 133).

2. If you want to, cut a fancy design on one side of the hatband. Find ideas in Fancy Edges (page 21).

3. Sew the hatband onto the hat with little dolphin running stitches (page 14). Add sequins, beads, or buttons if you like. See Adding Decorations (page 20) for help.

4. Choose small silk flowers and sequins (for the flower centers) for the hat. Start working from the backside of the hat, pushing the needle up through the felt, the flower, and then a sequin. Slide them down to rest on the felt. Push the needle back down next to the sequin. The sequin looks like the center of a flower and it also holds the petals in place. Beautiful!

5. Fold the hat in half and sew it up the back. For help, visit the hat shop (page 36). Add a few beads and a bell to the top if you want. Tie a knot and clip the threads. The fairy's hat is ready!

Finishing Your Fairy

1. If you want to give your fairy hair, follow the directions in Hair Studio (page 33). Lavender-and-turquoise hair is a springtime favorite!

2. Put a pinch of stuffing inside the hat. Add a dab of glue and put the hat on her head.

3. Let the glue dry. This fairy is ready for spring celebrating! Make more until you have your own fairy garden.

Making Your Spring Fairy Boy

Before you start, see if you have felt pieces big enough for the patterns you need to cut out. For this project you will use the Fairy shirt, pants, hat, hat topper, and hatband patterns (pages 132 and 133).

Face and Body

Make the fairy's body and face. Use one chenille stem for the legs and another for the arms. For help, see Faces Workshop (page 29) and Fairy Body Shop (page 27).

April Showers Fairy

Have you heard the saying, "April showers bring May flowers"?

The April Showers Fairy adores that idea! Spring is her favorite season, and when it's raining, it's even better! She loves to feel raindrops on her face, listen to rainfall pattering in the leaves, and even stomp in puddles, no matter what time of year! What do you love to do in the rain?

To make an April Showers Fairy girl, gnome, or boy, notice the colors on a rainy day—they are usually softer. You may see gray skies. Choose colors for your April Showers Fairy. Make your fairy just like Spring Fairy (page 52). When you decorate your hat, use the seed stitch to sew lots of raindrops on the hat. Learn about the seed stitch in the stitching workshop (page 13). Finish your fairy the same way as Spring Fairy.

Keep in mind your April Showers Fairy can't really get wet! What would be your favorite *indoor* rainy day activity you could do together? Read a book? Make more fairies and gnomes? Sit by a window and watch the rain falling? Rainy days are beautiful. April showers really do bring May flowers!

Making Your Spring Fairy Boy continued on page 58.

Clothes and Wings

1. Cut out felt using the Fairy pants pattern (page 132). Make pants and put them on the fairy following the directions in Pants and Shirt Shop (page 39). Then return here to make a shirt with petal or leaf wings.

2. Take apart the flower or leaves that you are using for the wings. Leaves may be on a flower stem. Learn more about flower petals and leaves in Things You Will Need, Flower Petals (page 10). Cut the ring of petals or set of leaves so that 2 petals or leaves are attached in the middle. These will be your fairy's wings. Be careful not to cut them apart.

3. Put the felt shirt on the fairy the same way you did the shirt for Fairy Boy (page 38). The petals or leaves become wings. Hold them against the fairy's back as you wind the thread. Tie off the thread with a double-knotted bow (page 18). Your fairy is almost ready to go fly in the garden!

Hat

1. Cut out felt using the Fairy hat pattern (page 133). Cut a wavy edge on the bottom of his hat. Learn about wavy lines in Fancy Edges (page 21).

2. Cut out felt using the Fairy hatband pattern (page 133). Place the band on different parts of the hat to see where you like it. If it's longer on the sides when you put it in the middle of the hat, clip the extra felt to match the edges of the triangle hat. Sew the band onto the hat with small dolphin running stitches (page 14). Add sequins if you want. For help, you can visit Adding Decorations (page 20).

3. Add a few extra sequins to decorate the rest of the hat if you like.

4. Cut out felt using the Fairy hat topper pattern (page 133), using the top of the hat pattern to make a tri-angle. Clip pointy ends onto the bottom edge of the triangle. Sew the top piece onto the hat.

5. When you are done decorating, sew up the back of the hat. For help, visit the hat shop (page 36). Your fairy is almost ready!

Finishing Your Fairy

1. Put a pinch of stuffing inside the hat. Add a dab of glue and put the hat onto his head.

2. Let the glue dry. Your fairy is ready for springtime! Draw a colorful garden scene together.

spring gnome

Making Your Spring Gnome

Before you start, see if you have felt pieces big enough for the patterns you need to cut out. For this project you will use the Gnome hat, hatband, body, and cape patterns (page 133). You will need 2 capes to make 1 gnome.

You Will Need

Makes 1 gnome.

- **1 piece of felt** for hat
- **1 piece of felt** for hatband
- **2 pieces of felt** for cape
- **1 piece of felt** for body
- **1 wood peg person** size 1¹¹⁄₁₆˝
- **Sequins**
- **1 tiny bell**
- **Thread**
- **Craft glue** (such as Aleene's Original Tacky Glue)

Body and Cape

1.
Cut out felt using the Gnome hat, hatband, body, and cape patterns (page 133). Cut out 1 hat, 1 hatband, 1 body, and 2 capes.

2.
Tie a thread around the felt on the gnome's body. For more directions, see Gnome (page 46). Wrap one end of the thread around the gnome's body a few times to look fancy. When you like how the gnome looks, tie the thread and clip the ends.

3.
Cut curves on the outside edge of 1 cape to look like petals. Cut curves on the other cape, too. Layer the capes on top of each other. Sew both layers of the cape on your gnome with a few stitches around the neck. For more help sewing gnome capes, see Gnome (page 46).

Hat

1.
Clip little ruffles on the top of the hatband (see Fancy Edges, page 21). Sew the gnome's hatband on the hat with a few dolphin running stitches, adding sequins as you sew. For help, see Adding Decorations (page 20).

2.
When the hat is finished, fold it in half and sew up the back. String a bead or bell (or both!) on the thread. For more help, visit the hat shop (page 36). Tie a knot and clip the thread.

Finishing Your Gnome

Put a dab of glue on the gnome's head to hold the hat in place. When the glue is dry, build a gnome home in the garden together!

Spring Fairies and Gnome   **59**

treasure pouch

FINISHED POUCH:
About 5˝ high

treasure pouch

Wandering in the garden is a wonderful way to spend a spring morning or afternoon. Along the way, you may find treasures like rocks or leaves that need safekeeping. Make a cute pouch so you can tuck them away until you get home and can display them on a nature-themed table or shelf.

You Will Need

Before you start, see if you have felt pieces big enough for the patterns you need to cut out. For this project you will use the Treasure Pouch pattern and your choice of butterfly or ladybug patterns (page 135).

- **1 piece of felt** at least 3″ × 8″ for pouch
- **Yarn or ribbon** for handle
- **Thread**
- **Perle cotton thread** for antennae (*if you want*)

BUTTERFLY

- **1 piece of felt** for butterfly wings
- **Scraps of felt** for butterfly body and decorations
- **Small silk flower**
- **1 button**

LADYBUG

- **1 piece of red felt** for ladybug body
- **1 piece of black felt** for ladybug head
- **Scraps of green felt** for leaves
- **Black sequins**

Making Your Pouch

For help with special stitches, visit the stitching workshop (page 13). For help with sewing on sequins and buttons, see Adding Decorations (page 20).

1. Cut out the pouch using the Treasure Pouch pattern (page 135).

CREATIVE IDEA

Make a pouch big enough for young children by enlarging the pattern. Decorate the front with buttons and felt shapes. Look for garden-themed buttons!

2. Fold the pouch into thirds. Lift the front pouch flap. Sew up one side of the pouch with the polar bear whipstitch or rabbit blanket stitch. Tie a knot and clip the threads. Do the same on the other side.

3. Make a handle for the pouch with ribbon or yarn. Sew the handle to the pouch using thread and making a few stitches on both sides. Tie bows, double knotting them so they don't come loose (see Double Bow, page 18).

Butterfly

1. Cut out the butterfly body and wings using the butterfly pattern pieces (page 135).

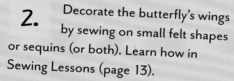

2. Decorate the butterfly's wings by sewing on small felt shapes or sequins (or both). Learn how in Sewing Lessons (page 13).

3. Sew the butterfly's body onto the center of the wings with a few dolphin running stitches.

4. To make butterfly antennae, tie a knot about ½˝ from the ends of the doubled thread. These ends will be the antennae. Put the needle through the front of the body where you want the first antenna to be. The knot should show on the front of your butterfly.

5. Push the needle back up through the felt where you want the second antenna to be. Clip the thread and tie the 2 threads together in a double knot (page 18). Trim them to be the same length as the first side.

6. Pick up the pouch. Pin the butterfly onto the front flap with a safety pin, checking that the butterfly is on the *outside* of the pouch, not the inside. Secure the butterfly with a few dolphin running stitches through the wings and the body. Be sure the flap is open before you sew! Take the safety pin off of the pouch. Don't clip the thread yet, though.

7. To sew on a flower with a button, bring the needle up through the back of the front flap and push the needle through the flower. Put the needle through one buttonhole. Push down both the flower and the button to rest against the felt. Then put the needle back down through the other buttonhole, flower, and felt again. Tie a knot in the back so the flower doesn't come loose. Clip the thread if you feel finished with your butterfly pouch. If you would like leaves, learn how to add them in Step 5 of the ladybug pouch (page 64).

1. Cut out the ladybug body and head using the ladybug pattern pieces (page 135). Cut out as many leaves as you want using the Small Leaf pattern (page 135).

2. Sew the head onto the ladybug with a few dolphin running stitches. Sew a line down the back using a manta ray backstitch.

3. Add spots to the ladybug using buttons or sequins. Give your ladybug antennae. See Butterfly, Steps 4 and 5 for help with antennae.

4. Sew the ladybug onto the front of the pouch using the same directions as Butterfly, Step 6.

5. Sew the leaves on with manta ray backstitches, making the stitches look like the veins in a leaf. Add sequins if you want. Push the thread to the bottom of the felt. Now it's time to tie the thread and clip it! Have fun collecting treasures for your new ladybug pouch.

CREATIVE IDEA

Design your own insect for a garden pouch. Think about the shapes and colors that you see. Draw ideas on paper before cutting felt. Be a pattern designer!

CREATIVE IDEA

Add an extra-fancy look to your pouch by sewing around the front flap with a rabbit blanket stitch.

lavender-scented mouse

SIZE: About 4˝ long before adding a tail

lavender-scented mouse

This mouse smells like lavender and loves to explore in the garden. The scent is calming to the forest critters and fairies. A wee mouse is a wonderful, cozy companion who loves to be with friends like you!

You Will Need

Before you start, see if you have felt pieces big enough for the patterns you need to cut out. For this project you will use the Lavender-Scented Mouse body, eye, nose, ears, and inner ear patterns (page 134). You will need 2 bodies, 2 eyes, and 2 inner ears to make 1 mouse.

- **1 piece of felt** for ears
- **Scraps of felt** for inner ears
- **Scrap of white felt** for eyes
- **Scrap of felt** for nose
- **2 pieces of felt** for body
- **2 small buttons** for eyes
- **Embroidery floss, ribbon, or yarn** for tail
- **1 small silk flower**
- **1 small decorative bead or button**
- **Dried lavender, cinnamon sticks, or tea bag**
- **Thread**
- **Stuffing**

Making Your Mouse

For help with special stitches, visit the stitching workshop (page 13).

1. Cut out felt using the Lavender-Scented Mouse body, eye, nose, ears, and inner ear patterns (page 134). Cut out 2 bodies, 2 eyes, 1 nose, 1 ears piece, and 2 inner ears.

2. Sew eyes onto the mouse. Start sewing from underneath the top piece of the mouse, pushing the needle through the body, the small white felt circle, and then through an eye button. Push the felt and button down the thread to rest on the mouse's body. Push the needle back down through another hole in the button. Tie off. Do the same thing with the other eye. For more help, see Sewing Lessons (page 13).

3. To sew the nose, start with the needle underneath the mouse. Sew the nose to the bottom part of the face with a few stitches.

4. Your mouse needs whiskers! Tie a knot about an inch or so from the ends of your thread. These threads will be the whiskers. Push your needle through the *front* side of the mouse's face where you want the whiskers to be.

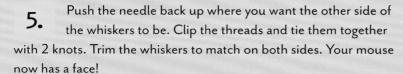

5. Push the needle back up where you want the other side of the whiskers to be. Clip the threads and tie them together with 2 knots. Trim the whiskers to match on both sides. Your mouse now has a face!

6. Sew the inner ear circles onto the ears using the dolphin running stitch.

7. Add ears to the mouse. Choose a little decoration to go in the middle of your mouse's ears, such as a little fabric flower and a button. Start the needle under the mouse's body. Push it up where you want the ears to be. Fold the ears in half lengthwise and push the needle through the narrow section of the ears.

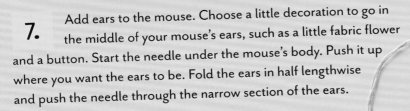

8. Push the needle through the middle of the flower and the bead or button. Press all the pieces down against the mouse's body. Push the needle back down through the flower, ears, and body. Now the bead or button is holding the ears on your mouse's head. Repeat the steps to make extra-strong stitches. Tie a knot underneath.

9. Line up the top and the bottom of the body. Sew around the outside edge with a polar bear whip-stitch or a rabbit blanket stitch. Leave an opening for stuffing.

10. Stuff the mouse until it's nice and puffy. Add dried lavender or a dry tea bag that smells nice. Sew the mouse shut.

11. Use a piece of ribbon or braid 3 strands of yarn for the tail. Tie a knot in the ribbon before tucking the tail between the pieces of felt so the ribbon doesn't unravel and come loose. Tuck the tail into the back of the mouse and secure with a few stitches. Tie a knot and clip the thread. The mouse is ready to be a calming new friend!

summer

Summer is the time that the sun is high, the water is cool, and the stars shoot through the sky. Summer invites you outside where fairies dance in the moonlight. On a hot summer afternoon, relax with a sewing activity.

summer fairies
and gnome

simple

FINISHED FAIRY:
About 5˝ high with hat

FINISHED GNOME: 3˝

summer fairies

Summer fairies love the sun!

You Will Need

To make 1 fairy, use the supplies listed under What Every Fairy Needs and either Fairy Girl or Fairy Boy.

WHAT EVERY FAIRY NEEDS

- **¾″ wood bead** for head
- **2 chenille stems** 12″ long for body
- **1 pair of silk flowers or leaves** for wings
- **Sequins and beads**
- **1 tiny bell** for hat
- **Thread**
- **A pinch of stuffing**
- **Craft glue** (such as Aleene's Original Tacky Glue)

FAIRY GIRL

- **1 piece of felt** for hat
- **1 piece of felt** for hatband
- **1 piece of felt** for shirt
- **1 piece of felt** for sun
- **Silk flower petals** for skirt
- **Yarn** for hair
- **1 button**

FAIRY BOY

- **1 piece of felt** for hat
- **3 pieces of felt** for hatbands
- **1 piece of felt** for shirt
- **1 piece of felt** for pants

Making Your Summer Fairy Girl

Before you start, see if you have felt pieces big enough for the patterns you need to cut out. For this project you will use the Fairy shirt, Fairy hat, Fairy hatband, and Sun patterns (pages 132, 133, and 141).

Face and Body

Make the fairy's body and face. Use one chenille stem for the legs and another for the arms. For help, see Faces Workshop (page 29) and Fairy Body Shop (page 27).

Summer Petal Dress and Wings

1. Cut out felt using the Fairy shirt pattern (page 132).

2. Clip petal shapes into the bottom of the fairy shirt. Put the fairy together using the directions in Flower Petal Skirt (page 54).

3. Glue the fairy's head onto the neck.

Hat

1. Cut out felt using the Fairy hat, Fairy hatband, and Sun patterns (pages 133 and 141).

2. On the felt circle, clip tiny triangles to make the edges look like rays of sunshine.

CREATIVE IDEA

The best way to cut out a tricky shape like the sun is to cut out each triangle shape separately. From the outside edge of the circle, cut a small diagonal line toward the center. Move the circle a bit and cut another diagonal to meet the first cut. That's a triangle! Continue around until the circle looks like a shining sun. You can learn more about cutting around shapes in Fancy Edges (page 21).

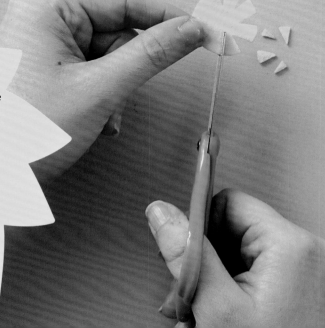

3. Start the needle on the back of the hat. Push the needle up through the hat, the sun, and the button. For help, see Adding Decorations (page 20). Use a few stitches to hold the sun on the fairy's hat if you want.

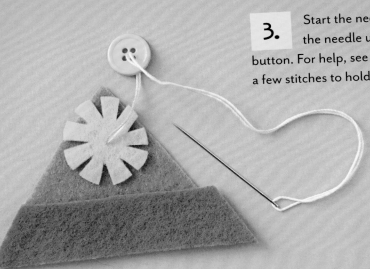

4. Clip ruffles along one side of the hatband so it looks like grass. Sew it onto the hat with a few dolphin running stitches (page 14). Add sequins as you sew if you want extra sparkles. Sew the hat together as shown in the hat shop (page 36).

Finishing Your Fairy

1. If you want to give your fairy hair, follow the directions in Hair Studio (page 33). Blue-and-orange hair is a summertime favorite!

2. Put a pinch of stuffing inside the hat. Add a dab of glue and put the hat on her head.

3. Let the glue dry. Your fairy is ready to play with you outside in the sunshine.

Summer Fairies and Gnome   75

Making Your Summer Fairy Boy

Before you start, see if you have felt pieces big enough for the patterns you need to cut out. For this project you will use the Fairy shirt, pants, hat, and hatband patterns (pages 132 and 133). You will need 3 hatbands to make 1 Summer Fairy Boy.

Face and Body

Make the fairy's body and face. Use one chenille stem for the legs and another for the arms. For help, see Faces Workshop (page 29) and Fairy Body Shop (page 27).

Clothes and Wings

1. Cut out felt using the Fairy shirt and pants patterns (page 132).

2. Make the pants the same way as the pants for the Fairy Boy. For directions, see Pants and Shirt Shop (page 39).

3. Put his shirt over the pants. Use leaves for his wings. For help with a shirt and leaf wings, follow the directions in Making Your Spring Fairy Boy, Clothes and Wings (page 58). Your fairy's outfit is fabulous!

4. Glue the fairy's head onto his neck.

Hat

1. Cut out felt using the Fairy hat and hatband patterns (page 133). Cut out 1 hat and 3 hatbands.

2. Pick up 1 hatband. Cut wavy lines along both edges. For help with wavy cutting, see Fancy Edges (page 21).

3. Cut a wavy edge along just one long side of each of the other 2 hatband pieces. Place all 3 hatbands on the hat to see where you like them. Sew them onto the hat one at a time with a dolphin running stitch (page 14). Add sequins, if you want.

4. If the hatband pieces are longer than the edges of the hat, trim the sides to match the hat's shape.

5. Fold the hat in half and sew up the back. Add a few beads and a bell. Use the hat shop (page 36) for help. Tie a knot and clip the thread.

Finishing Your Fairy

1. Put a pinch of stuffing inside the hat. Add a dab of glue and put the hat on his head.

2. Let the glue dry. Your fairy is ready to go for an evening walk and watch the stars come out!

Making Your Summer Gnome

Before you start, see if you have felt pieces big enough for the patterns you need to cut out. For this project you will use the Gnome cape, body, hat, and hatband patterns (page 133). You will need 2 capes and 2 hatbands for 1 gnome.

You Will Need

Makes 1 gnome.

- **1 piece of felt** for hat
- **2 pieces of felt** for hatbands
- **2 pieces of felt** for cape
- **1 piece of felt** for body
- **1 wood peg person** size 1¹¹⁄₁₆˝
- **Sequins and small beads** for hat
- **1 tiny bell**
- **Thread**
- **Craft glue** (such as Aleene's Original Tacky Glue)

Body and Cape

1. Cut out felt using the Gnome cape and body patterns. Cut out 2 capes from different colors and 1 body.

2. Tie a thread around the felt on the gnome's body. For more directions, see Gnome (page 46). Wrap one end of the thread around the gnome's body a few times. When you like how your gnome looks, tie the thread and clip the ends.

3. Cut a wavy line on the outside edge of 1 cape to look like water. Cut a wavy edge on the other cape, too. If you want help, see Fancy Edges (page 21). Layer the capes on top of each other. Sew both layers of the cape on your gnome with a few stitches around the neck. For help sewing capes, see Gnome (page 46).

Hat

1. Cut out felt using the Gnome hat and hatband patterns (page 133). Cut out 1 hat and 2 hatbands.

2. Cut along the hatbands to make wavy edges. Your summer gnome loves the water—but not for real. Your gnome can't go in real water.

3. Try the hatbands in a couple of different places on the hat. When you decide where to place them, trim the extra felt to match the edges of the hat.

4. Sew 1 hatband on the hat with dolphin stitches and sequins. For help, see Stitching Workshop (page 13) and Adding Decorations (page 20). Sew the other hatband on the hat the same way.

5. When the hat is finished, fold it in half and sew up the back. String a bead or a bell (or both!) onto the thread. See Hat Shop (page 36) for help. Tie a knot and clip the thread.

Finishing Your Gnome

Put a dab of glue on the gnome's head to hold the hat in place. Let the glue dry. Go enjoy a summer adventure together!

bride and groom fairies

FINISHED FAIRIES:
About 5˝ with hat

bride and groom fairies

Many brides and grooms get married in the summertime. These fairies are ready to walk down the aisle. You can have your very own fairy wedding party. They are also beautiful gifts to give a couple that you know is planning a wedding, and they look fantastic on top of a wedding cake!

You Will Need

Before you start, see if you have felt pieces big enough for the patterns you need to cut out. For this project, use either the Fairy shirt and hat patterns (pages 132 and 133) for the bride or the Groom Jacket, Fairy shirt, Fairy pants, Fairy hat, and Fairy hatband patterns (pages 132, 133, and 137) for the groom. If you are making both fairies, use all the patterns listed above. Makes 1 bride or 1 groom.

BRIDE

- **1 piece of white felt** for hat
- **1 piece of white felt** for shirt
- **White fabric flower petals** for skirt
- **¾˝ wood bead** for head
- **2 white chenille stems** 12˝ long for body
- **Yarn** for hair
- **1 piece of lacy ribbon** for hat
- **White sequins** for hat
- **1 tiny bell** for hat
- **Thread**
- **Small amount of stuffing** for hat
- **Craft glue** (such as Aleene's Original Tacky Glue)
- **Miniature wire flowers** for bouquet (*if you want*)

GROOM

- **1 piece of black felt** for hat
- **1 piece of ribbon** for hatband
- **1 piece gray felt** for jacket
- **1 piece of white felt** for shirt
- **1 piece of black felt** for pants
- **¾˝ wood bead** for head
- **1 chenille stem** 12˝ long for hands
- **1 chenille stem** 12˝ long for feet
- **1 tiny bell** for hat
- **Thread**
- **Small amount of stuffing** for hat
- **Craft glue** (such as Aleene's Original Tacky Glue)

TIP

A couple getting married would love to receive Bride and Groom fairies made in the same colors that will decorate the wedding. Match the thread, flower petals, or felt with the celebration colors and make a special gift!

Making Your Fairy

Face and Body

Make the fairy's body and face. Use one chenille stem for the legs and another for the arms. For help, see Faces Workshop (page 29) and Fairy Body Shop (page 27).

Bride

1. Cut a shirt for the top of the dress. Make a petal skirt for your bride. You can learn more in Flower Petal Skirt (page 54).

2. Cut a fairy hat for your bride. She loves lacy ribbon on her hat! Sew it with small stitches, and add iridescent or white sequins for extra sparkle. Finish sewing up the hat as explained in Hat Shop (page 36). Add a little heart charm to the top of the hat for extra love!

3. Put the Bride Fairy together. Use the hair studio (page 33) for help with hair. Your bride looks beautiful!

Groom

1. Cut out felt using the Fairy pants, Fairy shirt, Groom Jacket, and Fairy hat patterns (pages 132, 133, and 137).

2. Make the pants and shirt following the directions in Pants and Shirt Shop (page 39). Wrap the pants with black thread. Wrap the shirt with white thread. Your groom is getting dressed up for his big day!

3. The groom's jacket is a little formal and might be tricky. Cut the felt using the pattern. Clip the neck hole; then cut from the bottom edge to the neck hole on the front of the coat. The Groom jacket pattern shows where to cut.

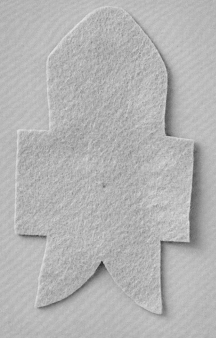

4. Fold the coat in half so the front matches the back on the sides. Use safety pins to hold it in place if you want. Thread a needle, and start sewing at the end of a sleeve. Use the polar bear whipstitch or rabbit blanket stitch to sew down one side. Tie off the thread. Make a new knot and sew the other side of the jacket the same way. Remove the safety pins. Your jacket is ready for the wedding!

5. Put the jacket on the groom. Add a dab of glue inside the wood bead for the head. Slide the head on his neck. If you want your fairy to have hair, glue it on the bead. Learn how in the hair studio (page 33).

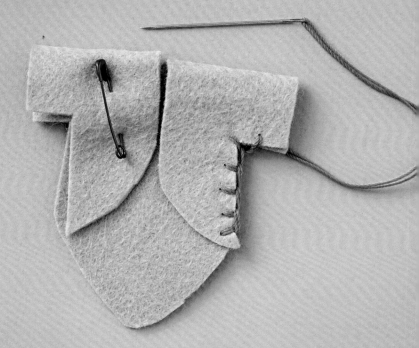

6. Sew the hat together using the directions in Hat Shop (page 36). You can add a special ribbon to make it unique for your groom. Add a dab of glue to hold the groom's hat on his head.

CREATIVE IDEA

Turn your bride and groom into a cake topper! To make an arch like the one in the big fairy wedding photo, use floral wire and a wood circle. Glue the fairies to the wood to help them stand up. We decorated our topper with miniature wired roses and bought our wooden base online at achildsdream.com.

Bride and Groom Fairies

shooting star beanbag
and rainbow ball

FINISHED BEANBAG/BALL: 4˜ before adding the tails

shooting star beanbag and rainbow ball

These beanbags are not only fun to make but also great for playing outdoor games! When the weather is nice, take them outside and play catch with a friend or toss them into buckets.

SHOOTING STAR BEANBAG

- **2 pieces of felt** for front and back
- **1 piece of felt** for decoration
- **Ribbons, yarn, or fabric strips**
- **Sequins**
- **Thread**
- **Dry beans and/or stuffing**
- **Stuffing**

RAINBOW BALL

- **4 pieces of felt** for sides of ball
- **Ribbons, yarn, or fabric strips**
- **Thread**
- **Dry beans and/or stuffing**
- **Stuffing**

Making Your Shooting Star Beanbag

Before you start, see if you have felt pieces big enough for the patterns you need to cut out. For this project you will use the Circle and Star or Heart patterns (page 136). You will need 2 circles to make 1 beanbag.

1. Cut out felt using the Circle and Star or Heart patterns. Cut out 2 circles for the front and back of the beanbag and 1 star shape or 1 heart shape.

2. Pin the star or heart shape onto the front circle with a safety pin to keep it from wiggling as you sew it in place. Push the needle up from under the felt through the circle and shape. You can add a sequin if you want—just don't add any heavy beads that could hurt if you are playing catch with someone. Push the needle back down through the shape and the felt. Sew more stitches to hold the shape onto the circle. Tie a knot on the back and clip the threads. Take off the safety pin.

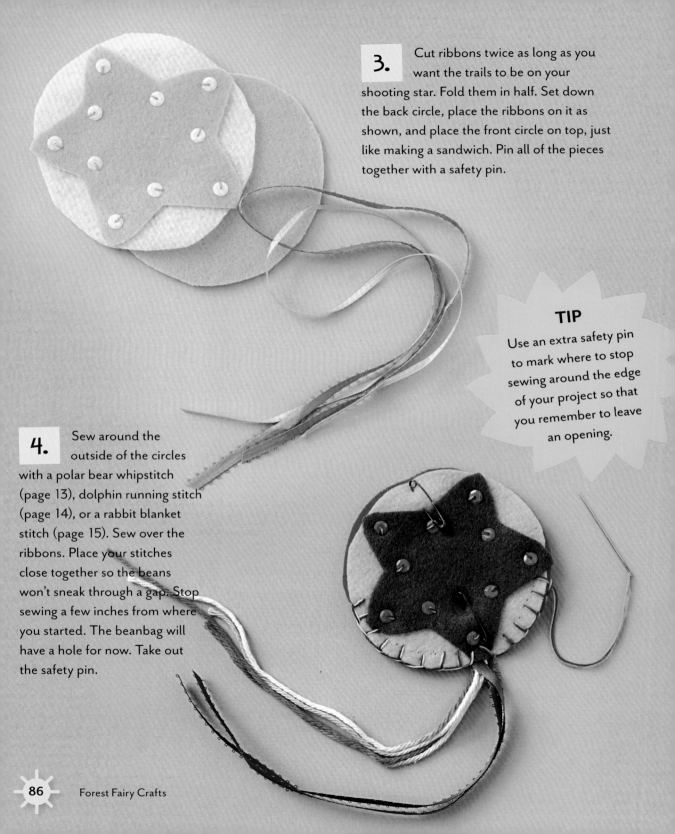

3. Cut ribbons twice as long as you want the trails to be on your shooting star. Fold them in half. Set down the back circle, place the ribbons on it as shown, and place the front circle on top, just like making a sandwich. Pin all of the pieces together with a safety pin.

TIP
Use an extra safety pin to mark where to stop sewing around the edge of your project so that you remember to leave an opening.

4. Sew around the outside of the circles with a polar bear whipstitch (page 13), dolphin running stitch (page 14), or a rabbit blanket stitch (page 15). Sew over the ribbons. Place your stitches close together so the beans won't sneak through a gap. Stop sewing a few inches from where you started. The beanbag will have a hole for now. Take out the safety pin.

5. Fill the small bag with beans. You can also add stuffing if you would like it to be puffier. Sew the opening shut with a few stitches. Tie a knot and clip the threads.

Your shooting star is ready for a game of catch. Throw it high, toss it far—shoot for the stars!

Shooting Star Beanbag and Rainbow Ball

Making Your Rainbow Ball

Before you start, see if you have felt pieces big enough for the patterns you need to cut out. For this project you will use the Large Leaf pattern (page 136). You will need 4 large leaves to make 1 ball.

1. Cut out felt using the Large Leaf pattern. Cut out 4 large leaves to make 1 rainbow ball. The pieces can all be a single color or mixed colors.

2. Sew together 2 large leaves. Start at the point and sew along an edge using a polar bear whipstitch (page 13) or rabbit blanket stitch (page 15). Keep the stitches short so that the beans you stuff inside later won't sneak out between stitches.

TIP

Use a safety pin to hold together felt pieces before sewing. Take it off when you are done with those sections.

3. Now you are ready for another section. Line it up on the unsewn edge of one of the pieces you already sewed together. It may seem a little tricky at first because it won't lie perfectly flat. The important thing is that the edges line up. Start sewing at one point and go around the outside edge to the other point.

4. Line up the last section of your ball. Insert it in the opening between the other pieces of felt. Make it match up at the edges the same way you did with the other pieces of felt. Sew that piece to the ball along one edge.

5. You should have one side left to line up and sew. Start at a point and sew just *halfway* up the side of the ball. Push some stuffing in your ball. Tuck it around the sides of the ball like a nest. Add a handful of beans and a little more stuffing until it's nicely puffy. Continue sewing along the edge to close the opening.

TIP
If there are gaps on the edge of the ball, sew them shut with a few stitches.

6. To make the tail, place ribbons, yarn, or strips of fabric—or a mix of them—in a neat pile. Pick up the strips at the halfway point and drape them over the ball, lining up the center of the strips with the ball at a spot where all the sections come together. Sew a few stitches across the center of the strips. Repeat the stitch a few times, going through all the layers. Tie off the thread with a good strong knot, and clip the thread.

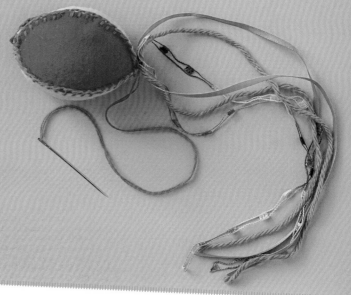

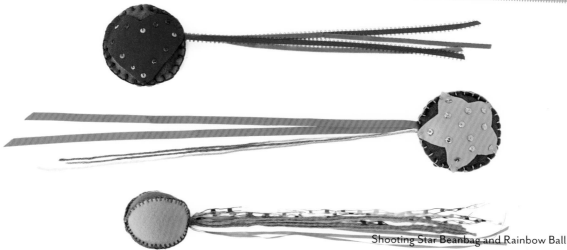

autumn

Autumn is beautiful in Fairyland. The trees sing, with colored leaves dancing in the breeze. As the air cools and the nights grow longer, fairies enjoy crisp apples and feasting with friends. They appreciate everything that surrounds them—their families and friends, curious critters, and the beauty of the forest. How do you celebrate Autumn? What are the colors of fall where you live? Reds, oranges, and browns inspire these Autumn Fairies.

autumn fairies
and gnome

FINISHED FAIRY:
About 5˝ high with hat

FINISHED GNOME: 3˝

autumn fairies

Making Your Autumn Fairy Girl

Before you start, see if you have felt pieces big enough for the patterns you need to cut out. For this project you will use the Fairy shirt, hat, and hatband patterns (pages 132 and 133). Use felt scraps for the tiny leaves.

Face and Body

Make the fairy's body and face. Use one chenille stem for the legs and another for the arms. For help, see Faces Workshop (page 29) and Fairy Body Shop (page 27).

You Will Need

To make 1 fairy, use the supplies listed under What Every Fairy Needs and either Fairy Girl or Fairy Boy.

WHAT EVERY FAIRY NEEDS

Find fabric leaves in decorative bouquets at the craft store—loose or on garlands. They may be called silk flowers.

- **¾″ wood bead** for head
- **2 chenille stems** 12″ long for body
- **Fabric autumn leaves** for wings
- **Thread**
- **A pinch of stuffing**
- **Craft glue** (such as Aleene's Original Tacky Glue)

FAIRY GIRL

- **1 piece of felt** for hat
- **1 piece of felt** for hatband
- **1 piece of felt** for shirt
- **Scraps of felt** for leaves on hat
- **Silk flower petals** for skirt
- **Yarn** for hair
- **Beads** for top of hat (can be shaped like leaves)
- **Sequins**
- **1 tiny bell**

FAIRY BOY

- **1 piece of felt** for shirt
- **1 piece of felt** for pants
- **1 acorn cap**

Clothes and Wings

1. Cut out felt using the Fairy shirt pattern (page 132).

2. Use fabric leaves in autumn colors for the wings. If 2 leaves are attached in the middle, use them just like petals (see Making Your Spring Fairy Girl, Spring Petal Dress Top and Wings, page 54). If the leaves are *not* attached, go to Step 3.

3. If the leaves are not attached, wrap the shirt on the fairy without wings. Tie a double bow (page 18) and clip the threads. Sew the leaves onto her back with a few little stitches. Bigger leaves can be folded in half before sewing them onto your fairy. Tie a knot and clip the thread.

4. Add petal skirts the same way as the summer petal dress and wings (page 74). Your autumn fairy looks fantastic!

Hat

For help with dolphin stitches, visit the stitching workshop (page 13). For help with sequins, see Adding Decorations (page 20).

1. Cut out felt using the Fairy hat and hatband patterns (page 133). Make a few little leaf shapes by cutting a rectangle and then cutting corners to be curves.

2. Place the hatband and felt leaves on the hat in different ways to see where you want them.

3. Put the leaves to the side for now. If you want the hatband in the middle of the hat, trim any extra felt on the sides. Sew the hatband on the hat with dolphin running stitches and sequins.

4. Push the needle up through the hat where you want to put a felt leaf. Push the needle through the leaf and slide it down to rest on the felt. Push the needle back down through the leaf and the hat. If you want veins, which are the little lines on a leaf, sew a couple of more stitches on the leaf.

5. Sew the rest of the leaves on the hat the same way. You can choose how many leaves you want.

6. When you are done adding leaves, fold the hat in half and sew it up the back. Add leaf-shaped beads and a bell to the top. Find help in the hat shop (page 36).

Finishing Your Fairy

1. Glue the head onto your fairy and give the fairy seasonal hair. Learn how in the hair studio (page 33). Autumn fairies love red, orange, and purple hair.

2. Put a pinch of stuffing inside the hat. Add a dab of glue and put the hat on the her head.

3. Let the glue dry, and your fairy is ready to dance in a pile of fallen leaves!

Autumn Fairies and Gnome

Making Your Autumn Fairy Boy

Before you start, see if you have felt pieces big enough for the patterns you need to cut out. For this project you will use the Fairy shirt and pants patterns (page 132).

Face and Body

Make the fairy's body and face. Use one chenille stem for the legs and another for the arms. For help, see Faces Workshop (page 29) and Fairy Body Shop (page 27).

Clothes and Wings

1. Cut out felt using the Fairy shirt and pants patterns (page 132). Make the pants using the directions in Pants and Shirt Shop (page 39).

2. Use fabric leaves in autumn colors for the wings. If 2 leaves are attached in the middle, use them just like petals and follow the directions in Making Your Spring Fairy Boy, Clothes and Wings (page 58). If the leaves are *not* attached, go to Step 3.

3. If the leaves are not together, wrap the shirt on the fairy without wings. Tie a double bow (page 18) and clip the threads. Sew the leaves with a few little stitches on his back. Bigger leaves can be folded in half before sewing them onto your fairy. Tie a knot and clip the thread. Your fairy looks dashing!

Hat

Use an acorn cap for the fairy's hat. Find fallen acorns under old trees near your home, at a park, or even by a building. Take a few acorn caps home. Choose an acorn cap that looks good on your fairy!

Finishing Your Fairy

1. Glue the fairy's head onto the neck.

2. Add a dab of glue inside the acorn cap and put it on the fairy's head. Let the glue dry. Your fairy is ready to help you collect more acorns!

CREATIVE IDEA

While making your fairy, think of all of the things that you are grateful for in the world. Make a little book to read with your fairy.

I am thankful for my family ♡

autumn gnome

Making Your Autumn Gnome

Before you start, see if you have felt pieces big enough for the patterns you need to cut out. For this project you will use the Gnome body and cape patterns (page 133).

You Will Need

Makes 1 gnome.

- **1 piece of felt** for hat
- **1 piece of felt** for hatband
- **2 pieces of felt** for cape
- **1 piece of felt** for body
- **1 wood peg person** size 1$\frac{11}{16}$˝
- **Sequins**
- **1 tiny bell**
- **Thread**
- **Craft glue** (such as Aleene's Original Tacky Glue)

Body and Cape

1. Cut out felt using the Gnome cape and body patterns (page 133). Choose harvest colors for the gnome, such as warm oranges and yellows or deep burgundies and browns.

2. Tie a thread around the felt on your gnome's body. For more directions, see Gnome (page 46). Wrap one end of the thread around the gnome's body a few times. When you like how your gnome looks, tie the thread and clip the ends.

3. Sew the cape on the gnome with a few stitches around the neck. For help sewing capes, see Gnome (page 46).

Hat

1. Our autumn gnome wears an acorn cap. We found an acorn with part of the branch still attached. Try different acorn caps to see which one fits and looks good on your gnome. Learn more about acorn caps in Things You Will Need (page 9).

2. Your gnome can wear a felt hat instead. Use fall colors and see the directions in Gnome (page 46). Add a leaf, or several, to match the Fairy Girl if you want.

Finishing Your Gnome

Put a dab of glue on the gnome's head to hold the hat in place. Let the glue dry. Now go make a gnome home from fallen leaves!

Autumn Fairies and Gnome   **99**

tricky

chubby critters

FINISHED CRITTERS:
About 4˝ high

chubby critters

When you wander in the forest, these little friends may follow you home. They adore romping around neighborhoods and delight in playing with fairies!

CAT

- **1 piece of black felt** for front
- **1 piece of black felt** for back
- **1 piece of black felt** for bottom
- **1 piece of black felt** for tail
- **Scraps of felt** for nose, cheeks, ears, and paws
- **2 buttons**
- **Thread**
- **Perle cotton thread** for whiskers
- **Stuffing**

FOX

- **1 piece of orange felt** for front
- **1 piece of orange felt** for back
- **1 piece of orange felt** for bottom
- **1 piece of orange felt** for tail
- **Scraps of white felt** for face, ears, paws, and tail tuft
- **Scrap of brown felt** for nose
- **2 buttons**
- **Thread**
- **Stuffing**

CREATIVE IDEA

Make any Chubby Critter into a pillow by sewing together the front and back pieces, without adding a bottom piece. After sewing the cat or fox around the sides, continue sewing along the bottom edge, but leave an opening. Stuff the project when you have a few inches left. Then sew up the opening, tie a knot, and clip the threads. Great for young children!

Making Your Chubby Cat

Before you start, see if you have felt pieces big enough for the patterns you need to cut out. For this project you will use the Chubby Critter front, back, bottom, ear inserts, paws, cat nose, cat cheeks, and cat tail patterns (pages 137 and 138). You will need 2 ear inserts and 2 paws to make 1 Chubby Cat. For help with special stitches, visit the stitching workshop (page 13).

1. Cut out felt using the Chubby Critters front, back, bottom, ear inserts, paws, cat nose, cat cheeks, and cat tail patterns. Remember to cut 2 paws and 2 ear inserts!

2. Make a face for the cat, starting with the eyes. The front piece is the piece without ears; start with the needle on the back of this piece. Push the needle up through the felt. Thread the needle through a button, and move the button down the thread until it's against the cat felt. Put the needle down through another button and the cat's body. The needle will be at the back of the felt. If you have more holes in the button, sew through them, too. Tie a knot and clip the thread. Sew on the other eye the same way. See Adding Decorations (page 20) for more directions about sewing buttons if you need more help.

3. The nose and cheeks are next. Stitch them onto the face with a few dolphin running stitches through the nose.

4. Let's give the cat whiskers. Thread the needle, double the threads, and tie a knot a little distance from the thread ends. Start the needle on the front of the cat and push it through a cheek. The thread ends become the whiskers! Bring the needle back up through the other cheek and clip the needle off of the thread, leaving long ends. Tie a double knot (page 18) with the 2 thread ends. Trim the threads to match the length of the other whiskers. Add as many sets of whiskers as you like.

5. Sew paws onto your cat, holding them in place with safety pins if you want. Sew claws onto the paws using a few up-and-down dolphin running stitches. Sew a few more stitches around the edges of the paw. Take off the safety pins if you used them.

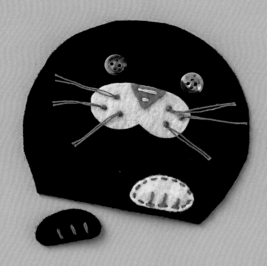

6. Now we make the ears! Pick up the back piece of felt. Add the triangle shapes inside the ears by sewing them in place with a few stitches. Tie off the thread and clip the ends.

7. Sew the cat together by lining up the front and the back body pieces. Use a safety pin to help them stay in place. Starting at a bottom corner, sew up and around the top of the cat to the other bottom corner. Use the polar bear whipstitch or the rabbit blanket stitch—except by the ears. Use the dolphin running stitch by the cat's ears. Leave the flat part along the bottom of the cat open. Take out the safety pin.

8. To sew on the bottom piece, line it up with the opening at the bottom of the cat. Stitch around the bottom edge of the cat using a polar bear whipstitch or rabbit blanket stitch, leaving a little gap to put stuffing inside. Fill your cat with stuffing. Sew the opening shut. Tie a knot and clip the threads.

9. Sew the cat's tail onto the back of the cat using the dolphin running stitch. Sew it along the bottom edge. If you want the tail to stand up, sew a few dolphin running stitches through the middle of the tail and into the center of the back. Be careful. You don't want to push your needle all the way through the front of the cat.

TAIL TIP

Sew a tail to a Chubby Critter by pushing the needle down and then pushing it back up, all in one move. Go down with the point of the needle and push it right back up; then pull the needle through the felt.

10. After you have enough stitches to hold the cat's tail in place, tie a knot and clip the threads.

Meow! Your cat is ready to play!

Making Your Chubby Fox

Before you start, see if you have felt pieces big enough for the patterns you need to cut out. For this project you will use the patterns for the Chubby Critter front, back, bottom, ear inserts, paws, fox face, fox nose, fox tail, and fox tail tuft patterns (pages 137–139). You will need 2 ear inserts and 2 paws to make 1 Chubby Fox. For help with all the special stitches, visit the stitching workshop (page 13).

1. Cut out felt using the Chubby Critter front, back, bottom, ear inserts, paws, fox face, fox nose, fox tail, and fox tail tuft patterns. Remember to cut 2 paws and 2 ear inserts!

2. Make a foxy face! Sew the white V-shaped face piece onto the top of the front piece, which is the body piece without ears. Use a dolphin running stitch to sew around the outside edges of the V-shaped face.

3. Add 2 buttons for the eyes. Sew them onto the white V shape. See Adding Decorations (page 20) for help with sewing buttons. Add the nose to the bottom of the V shape with a few dolphin running stitches.

4. Follow Steps 5–8 of Making Your Chubby Cat (pages 103 and 104) to add claws, paws, and ear inserts. Sew the fox together.

5. Let's make a tail for your fox! Overlap the white tail tuft felt with the end of the tail a little bit. Sew those pieces together with a few stitches.

6. Decide if you want the fox's tail to stay up or be loose. Attach the bottom of the tail to the bottom of the fox with a dolphin running stitch. For a tail that stays up, attach it to the middle of the fox's back with a few stitches. Read the tail tip (page 105) for a great way to do this. Give the fox's tail a little curve by bending the tail and then making the stitches. The tail will curl like the one in the photograph. Tie off the thread and clip it.

Your critter is ready to play foxy games!

simple leaf garland

leaf garland

Fall is a time when the trees sing with color. Green leaves turn yellow, orange, red, and deep purple. Notice how the colors change. Celebrate the season with a beautiful string of leaves that's fun to create.

Making Your Garland

Before you start, see if you have felt pieces big enough for the patterns you need to cut out. For this project you will use the Large Leaf pattern (page 136). Choose how many leaves you would like to string together.

(page 136)

You Will Need

- **Scraps of felt** for leaves in a variety of autumn colors
- **Sequins and/or beads**
- **Thread**

1. Cut out felt using the Large Leaf pattern. Start with 4–6 leaves. You can always add more!

2. Tie a knot on the thread. Sew up and down the center of the leaf using a dolphin running stitch. As you make a stitch, add a bead or a sequin on both sides of the leaf. For help with sequins, see Adding Decorations (page 20).

(page 20)

3. When you reach the end of the leaf, continue sewing through to the next leaf, adding more stitches with sequins as you go. Do not pull the thread too tight or the leaves will bunch up in a heap by the knot. Instead sew gently, trying to keep the thread flat through each leaf.

4. When you are done with your last leaf, tie a knot and clip the threads. The leaf garland is ready to drape over a photo, around a display of autumn treasures, or in a window, creating the look of falling leaves.

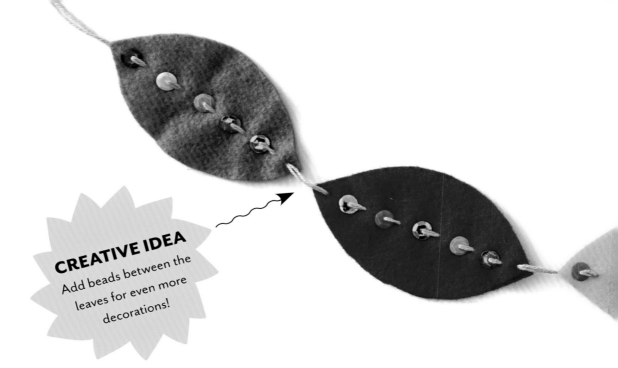

CREATIVE IDEA
Add beads between the leaves for even more decorations!

Making Your Own Pattern

You can create a garland of your own design! Draw a shape on paper and cut it out. This is your pattern! Trace the shape onto all colors of felt; then cut these out. String the shapes together, and you have a unique, one-of-a-kind garland!

CREATIVE IDEA

Celebrate year-round with garlands made from different shapes. Make hearts, green leaves, puffy clouds, stars, or raindrops. Make a garland with circles to show snowballs. Or make suns, moons, or butterflies. Sew fabric flower blossoms between green leaves for a springtime look. What shape can you turn into a garland?

Leaf Garland

winter

As the days get shorter, fairies light up a hundred tiny, colorful lights to shine in the darkness of winter. They decorate trees; they light candles that reflect in the snow. Celebrate the season by making your own wintry friends.

simple

winter fairies
and gnome

FINISHED FAIRY:
About 5˝ high with hat

FINISHED GNOME: 3˝

winter fairies

You Will Need

To make 1 fairy, use the supplies listed under *What Every Fairy Needs* and either *Fairy Girl* or *Fairy Boy*.

WHAT EVERY FAIRY NEEDS

- **¾˝ wood bead** for head
- **2 chenille stems** 12˝ long for body
- **Wired ribbon** for wings
- **Snowflake-shaped sequins**
- **Sequins and/or beads**
- **1 tiny bell** for hat
- **Thread**
- **Tiny bit of stuffing** for inside the hat
- **Craft glue** (such as Aleene's Original Tacky Glue)

FAIRY GIRL

- **1 piece of felt** for hat
- **1 piece of felt** for hatband
- **1 piece of felt** for shirt
- **Petal flowers** for skirt
- **Yarn** for hair

FAIRY BOY

- **1 piece of felt** for hat
- **1 piece of felt** for hatband
- **1 piece of felt** for shirt
- **1 piece of felt** for pants

Making Your Winter Fairy Girl

Before you start, see if you have felt pieces big enough for the patterns you need to cut out. For this project you will use the Fairy shirt, hat, and icicle hatband patterns (pages 132, 133, and 141).

Face and Body

Make the fairy's body and face. Use one chenille stem for the legs and another for the arms. For help, see Faces Workshop (page 29) and Fairy Body Shop (page 27).

Clothes and Wings

1. Cut out felt using the Fairy shirt pattern (page 132).

2. Follow the directions in the dress shop (page 31) to make the fairy's shirt with ribbon wings.

3. Give a her petal skirt. Winter skirts can be pale blue and white, like chilly mornings. For help with petal skirts, see Flower Petal Skirt (page 54) for directions. Your fairy can be a snow queen!

4. Glue the fairy's head onto her neck, and add hair if you want. Visit the hair studio (page 33) to learn how.

Hat

1. Cut out felt using the Fairy hat and icicle hatband patterns (pages 133 and 141).

2. Make the hatband look like icicles by cutting a diagonal line into the top of the hatband. Move over just a bit and cut another line to meet the first line, making a thin triangle. Continue across the hat so it looks like icicles. For help, visit Fancy Edges (page 21).

3. Start the thread under the hat. Push the needle up through the hat and icicle hatband. Add a sequin; then push the needle back down through the hatband and hat. Continue across.

4. Push the needle up in the center of the hat. String a snowflake-shaped sequin or a button on the thread. Push the needle back down. Tie a knot and clip the threads.

5. Fold the hat in half. Sew the hat together up the back of the hat. Visit the hat shop (page 36) if you would like help. Tie a knot and clip the threads.

Finishing Your Fairy

1. Put a pinch of stuffing inside the hat. Add a dab of glue and put the hat on the her head.

2. Let the glue dry. The fairy is ready to enjoy a winter celebration with you!

Making Your Winter Fairy Boy

Before you start, see if you have felt pieces big enough for the patterns you need to cut out. For this project you will use the Fairy shirt, pants, hat, and icicle hatband patterns (pages 132, 133, and 141).

Face and Body

Make the fairy's body and face. Use one chenille stem for the legs and another for the arms. For help, see Faces Workshop (page 29) and Fairy Body Shop (page 27).

Clothes and Wings

1. Cut out felt using the Fairy shirt and pants patterns (page 132).

2. Make the pants and shirt the same way as the pants for the Fairy Boy. Use ribbon for his wings. For help, follow the directions in Pants and Shirt Shop (page 39).

3. Glue the fairy's head onto his neck.

Hat and Finishing Your Fairy

Both winter fairies wear the same style of hat. To make their hats, follow the directions for Making Your Winter Fairy Girl, Hat (previous page). Your fairy looks like Jack Frost!

winter gnome

The winter gnome lives in the mountains. His hat has a mountain theme. We chose gray and white felt to look like mountains and snow.

You Will Need

Makes 1 gnome.

- **1 piece of felt** for hat
- **1 piece of felt** for hatband
- **2 pieces of felt** for cape
- **1 piece of felt** for body
- **1 scrap of white felt** for snow on top of hat
- **1 wood peg person** size 1¹¹⁄₁₆˜
- **1 tiny bell**
- **Thread**
- **Craft glue**

Making Your Winter Gnome

Before you start, see if you have felt pieces big enough for the patterns you need to cut out. For this project you will use the Gnome body, cape, hat, hatband, and hat snow patterns (pages 133 and 141). You will need 2 capes to make 1 Winter Gnome.

Body and Cape

1. Cut out felt using the Gnome body and cape patterns (page 133). Cut out 1 body and 2 capes.

2. Tie a thread around the felt on the gnome's body. For more directions, see Gnome (page 46). Wrap one end of the thread around the gnome's body a few times. When you like how your gnome looks, tie the thread and clip the ends.

3. Cut triangles into the felt on the outside edge of one cape to look like icicles. To do that, snip into the felt just a bit. Then scoot along the felt a tiny bit, and cut another line to meet the first line. You cut a triangle! Make more thin triangles around the cape. Learn more about decorative cutting in Fancy Edges (page 21).

TIP: DRAW FIRST

Draw icicle shapes on the felt first with a marker to see where to cut.

4. Cut out icicle shapes on the other cape, too.

5. Layer the capes on top of each other. Sew both layers of the cape on your gnome with a few stitches around the neck. For more help sewing capes, see Gnome (page 46).

Hat

1. Cut out felt using the Gnome hat, hatband, and hat snow patterns (pages 133 and 141).

2. Sew the snow to the top of the hat with a few dolphin running stitches (page 14). Looks like winter is coming!

3. Cut triangles into the hatband. Sew the hatband onto the hat using dolphin running stitches.

4. Fold the hat in half. Sew it together. Visit the hat shop (page 36) for more help. Add a bell. Tie a knot and clip the threads.

Finishing Your Gnome

Put a dab of glue on the gnome's head to hold the hat in place. Let the glue dry. Your Winter Gnome is ready build an igloo with you— or maybe a fort in the living room!

simple

lovely
ornaments

lovely ornaments

Creating decorations during the holiday season is fun for many reasons. It's fun to sit and craft with people that you love. It's fun to hang up crafts as decorations for a home or a tree. And it's fun to wrap gifts and give them to special people in your life. These ornaments give you the chance to do all of those things! Add your creative flair to make your ornament especially festive.

You Will Need

Before you start, see if you have felt pieces big enough for the patterns you need to cut out. For this project you will use the Circle pattern (page 136). You will need 2 circles—one for the front and one for the back— to make 1 ornament.

- **2 pieces of felt** for front and back
- **Sequins, buttons, and/or beads**
- **Thread**
- **Stuffing**
- **1 piece of felt or fabric** for decoration (*if you want*)
- **Fabric flowers for decoration** (*if you want*)
- **Cinnamon stick, dry herbs, or tea bag** for scented ornament (*if you want*)

Making Your Lovely Ornament

Choose which style of ornament that you wish to sew. Add a tree or a star shape to the front, or use beads to create a snowflake pattern or another festive design.

Cut out felt using the Circle pattern (page 136). Cut out 2 circles for the front and back of your ornament.

TIP
A very young crafter might enjoy sewing beads and sequins to felt without fussing about a pattern or plan. Freedom can be fun!

Shapes: Star or Tree

1. Cut out felt using the Lovely Ornaments star or tree pattern (page 140).

2. Place the shape on one of the felt circles. Hold it in place with a safety pin. Start sewing from the back. Push the needle up through the felt and add a bead or sequin. This will hold the shape in place.

3. Add a sequin border around the edge of the circle if you want. See Adding Decorations (page 20) for help. Tie a knot on the back and clip the thread. Take the safety pin off. You can decorate the other side of your ornament, too, if you like.

4. Follow the directions in Finishing Your Lovely Ornament (next page).

CREATIVE IDEA

Make ornaments with other shapes to celebrate other holidays and seasons. Sew a red heart on a pink circle for Valentine's Day, a fabric flower and bright bead on a green circle to celebrate spring, a shining sun for summer, or fall leaves for autumn.

Snowflake

1. Use the dolphin running stitch and sequins to create a snowflake pattern on your ornament. If you want, you can plan your design on piece of paper. Think of how snowflakes have lines and patterns. You can make the lines with dolphin stitches or manta ray stitches (pages 14 and 16) and sequins.

2. Sew a border with sequins around the edge of the snowflake. Your sparkly snowflake looks wonderful! Tie off the thread on the back and clip away the needle. You can decorate the other side, too, if you like.

3. Follow the directions for finishing your Lovely Ornament (below).

Finishing Your Lovely Ornament

1. Line up the front and back of your ornament. Use a safety pin to hold them together if you want. Sew around the edges with a polar bear whipstitch or rabbit blanket stitch (pages 13 and 15). Stop when you have a few inches left. Take off the safety pin if you used one.

2. Add stuffing to your ornament. Include something scented if you like. Finish sewing around the edge, closing the gap shut.

3. Add a loop of thread or a bit of ribbon to the top for hanging the ornament.

CREATIVE IDEA
Make your ornament smell wonderful by adding dry herbs, cloves, a cinnamon stick, or a tea bag inside. Your ornament can be scented like the season. Just be careful that your scented ornament never gets wet, or the tea or herbs will stain the felt!

Your ornament is finished!
Go hang it up or wrap it
with pretty paper to give to
someone you love.

CREATIVE IDEA

Ornaments make great decorations
long after Christmas has passed.
They can be hung in windows with
a long beaded thread. Or they can
be made into a mobile. Winter
projects celebrate a season long
after the holiday passes.

CREATIVE IDEA

These crafts can be decorated for many winter celebrations. Choose different colors for different occasions, such as blue and silver for Hanukkah; red and white for Saint Nicholas Day; pale blue and white for winter solstice; or black, red, and green for Kwanzaa. Decorate your home with heartfelt crafts, and make a few more to give to family, friends, and teachers. Or donate to your favorite causes!

sweetheart fairy baby
and heart home

FINISHED FAIRY: About 4˜ high with hat

sweetheart fairy baby and heart home

The sweetest little fairies in the forest sleep in heart-shaped homes. You can carry a sweetheart fairy wherever you go—best friends travel together! These also make heartfelt gifts for friends.

You Will Need

Makes 1 fairy and 1 home.

SWEETHEART FAIRY BABY

- **1 piece of felt** for hat
- **1 piece of felt** for body
- **Scrap of felt** for heart decoration
- **½˝ wood bead** for head
- **1 chenille stem** clipped to 6˝ long for body frame
- **1 little button**
- **1 tiny pom-pom** for hat
- **Thread**
- **Stuffing**
- **Craft glue**

HEART HOME

- **1 piece of felt** for front
- **1 piece of felt** for back
- **Scraps of green felt** for leaves
- **2 fabric flowers** for decoration
- **1 button**
- **Thread**

Making Your Sweetheart Fairy Baby

Before you start, see if you have felt pieces big enough for the patterns you need to cut out. For this project you will use the Fairy Baby body and Sweetheart Fairy Baby hat patterns (pages 133 and 141).

Clothes

1. Cut out felt using the Fairy Baby body pattern (page 133).

2. Sew a special button to the front of your Sweetheart Fairy Baby body. For help with sewing on a button, see Adding Decorations (page 20).

3. Put the Sweetheart Fairy Baby together using the directions in Fairy Baby (page 42). Tie a knot and clip the threads. Add a dab of glue inside the baby's head and put it onto the neck.

Hat

1. Cut out felt using the Sweetheart Fairy Baby hat pattern (page 141).

2. This fairy's hat is an upside-down heart. Turn the heart upside down before adding decorations. Sew a sequin, button, or tiny felt piece to the front of the hat. If you sew on a shape, use a dolphin running stitch (page 14) to hold it in place.

3. Fold the hat in half. Start sewing where the heart curves around. You can always test the spot by pinching the hat together and trying it on your fairy's head. Sew your hat using directions in the hat shop (page 36). Use the polar bear whipstitch or rabbit blanket stitch. You can add a tiny flower and bell or pom-pom to the top. Tie a knot. You can hide your tails by sewing into the hat and clipping the threads.

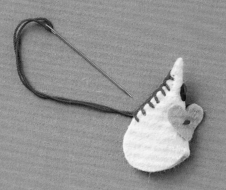

4. Add a dab of glue to the Sweetheart Fairy Baby hat and put it on the baby's head. Let the glue dry.

Make a heart-shaped bed for your Sweetheart Fairy Baby!

Making Your Heart Home

Before you start, see if you have felt pieces big enough for the patterns you need to cut out. For this project you will use the Heart Home front, Heart Home back, and Small Leaf patterns (pages 135, 140, and 141).

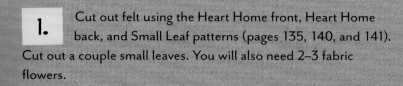

1. Cut out felt using the Heart Home front, Heart Home back, and Small Leaf patterns (pages 135, 140, and 141). Cut out a couple small leaves. You will also need 2–3 fabric flowers.

2. Let's make the front of the bed beautiful! The front is the smaller piece. Sew on the leaves using a single dolphin running stitch or a few manta ray backstitches (page 16).

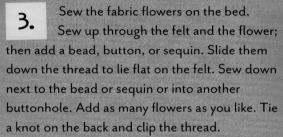

3. Sew the fabric flowers on the bed. Sew up through the felt and the flower; then add a bead, button, or sequin. Slide them down the thread to lie flat on the felt. Sew down next to the bead or sequin or into another buttonhole. Add as many flowers as you like. Tie a knot on the back and clip the thread.

4. Sew the front and back together. Use a safety pin to hold the pieces together if you want. Start sewing on one side of the heart. Use the polar bear whipstitch or rabbit blanket stitch. Sew around to the other side of the heart. Tie a knot and clip the threads. Remove the safety pin if you used one.

The heart is a lovely bed ready for sweet(heart) dreams. Tuck the fairy baby inside for a nap.

Sweetheart Fairy Baby and Heart Home

Notes for Adults

Tips and Tricks for Crafting with Children

Children appreciate help with sewing, especially at first. Children under the age of eight will probably want you to sit with them for their first few sewing crafts. What a lovely chance to spend time together! All children are different and have different skills. They will also contribute delightful ideas to every project.

Here are a few ideas to help your child sew:

Hold the felt: Beginning crafters concentrate all of their attention on the stitching. That needle is sharp! They may use one hand to push the needle through the felt and reach with the other hand to pull the thread tight. When you hold the felt for them, they can focus on the sharp needle. They will let you know when they are ready to hold the felt themselves by asking or reaching for it on their own.

Let them see the needle: Children can be very invested in the sharp end of the needle. At first, it's hard for them to imagine where the needle will come up out of the felt. They may turn the felt to keep pushing the needle "down" where they can see it. We've seen children tip their head to see under the felt. That's why the polar bear whipstitch goes down instead of coming up through the felt. At some point, children will begin to see and will start pushing their needle up through the felt more. Until they grow developmentally and can visualize where the needle will appear from underneath the felt, you can support them by letting them choose which way is comfortable.

Finish the knots: Younger children find knots tricky. Having a project fall apart is not fun, so your help is wonderful.

Trace and cut the patterns: Some younger children do not have the fine motor skills to trace, hold, and cut felt with scissors—especially on small, tricky shapes. Let them choose the colors. Then you can cut out the shapes!

Double and knot the thread ends: Children will pull the needle off with every stitch if you don't tie the ends together. They may also sew until they have no thread to make a knot. Teach them to stop sewing with a few inches left so you can tie a knot. Some will sew until the needle will no longer move!

Be available: As they gain confidence, children may not need directed help, but they still appreciate having you nearby in case of difficulties. Try not to jump in at the first sign of trouble. Wait to be asked for assistance. You may sew your own project while they sew theirs. When you step back, children learn persistence, resilience, and creative problem-solving. Their solutions will surprise you.

Encourage inspiration: Children adore the creative process—invite them to create their own patterns or crafts! They can draw ideas and plan how to craft something from start to finish. Take crafts to the next level! Add paint, beaded crowns, miniature wands, and more.

Love the results: Cherish "mistakes." Too quickly, a child's crafting becomes tidy. Enjoy the exuberance of long stitches and overlapping threads. Children love their crafts, and they thrive on validation from you. A magical craft captures a child's personality. Celebrate their creativity!

Photo by Lenka Vodicka-Paredes

Crafting with Groups of Children

Whether crafting at a birthday party, in a classroom, with a scout troop, or during a visit with friends, there are many ways to sew with multiple children and have fun together. Being prepared is *so* helpful. To work with a group, cut your felt ahead of time. Cut extras so everyone gets to choose their color—even the last, most patient child. Thread your needles beforehand as well.

Write names on tape to identify and store the crafts. When children go home, they can take the tape off of their craft.

Try not to make children wait in lines. Older children who need help can write their name on a list and go color or read a book while waiting. Younger children can leave their project in a line to hold their place, and you can call them up when you are ready to help. You can always have a basket where they can put their completed sewing so you can tie finished knots later.

Remember that children express themselves with many, many ideas. From the minimalist single sequin to the super-sequined hat, each creation should reflect its crafter. Take a photograph of all the crafts together. You will be amazed at what your group can create!

Patterns

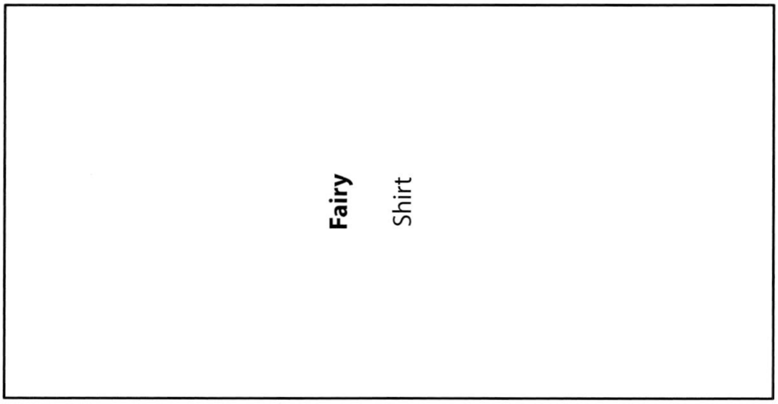

Fairy
Shirt

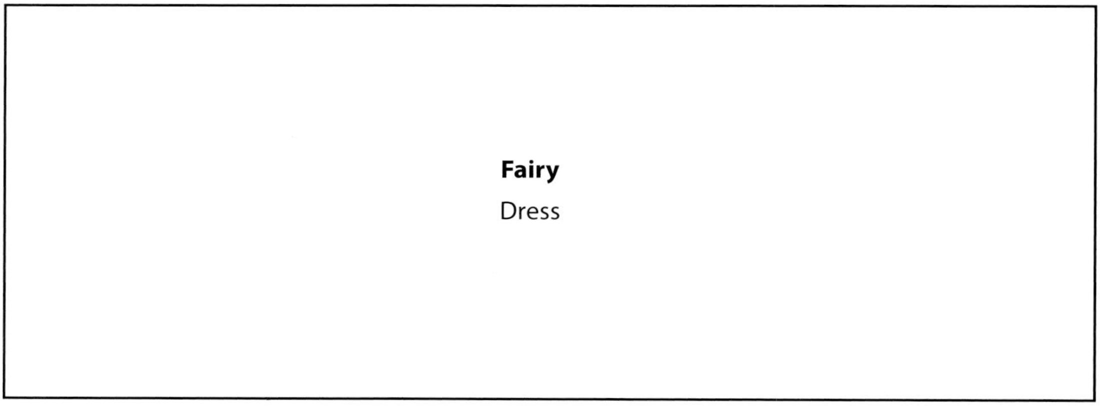

Fairy
Dress

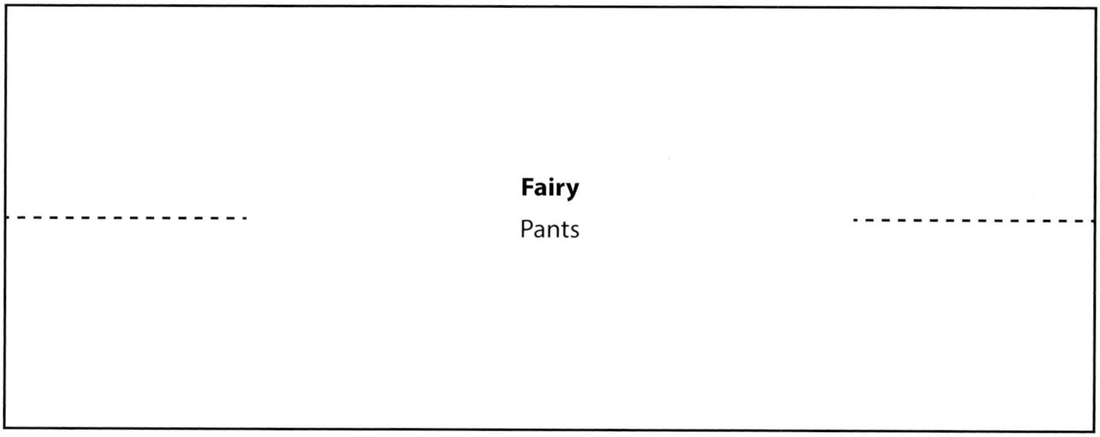

Fairy
Pants

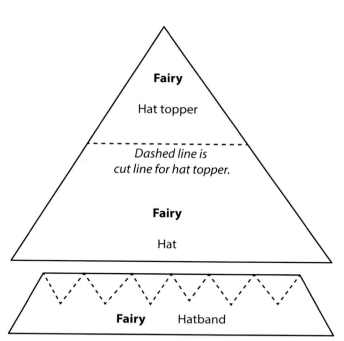

Fairy

Hat topper

*Dashed line is
cut line for hat topper.*

Fairy

Hat

Fairy   Hatband

Dashed lines are suggested cuts.

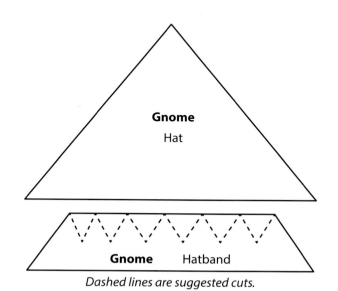

Gnome
Hat

Gnome   Hatband

Dashed lines are suggested cuts.

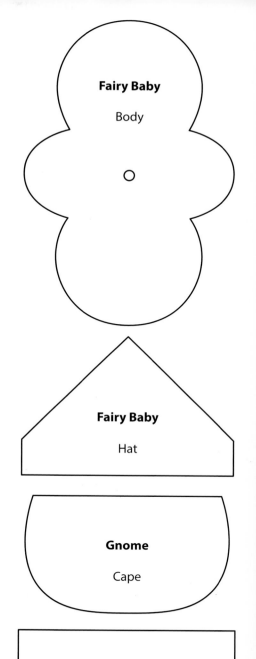

Fairy Baby

Body

Fairy Baby

Hat

Gnome

Cape

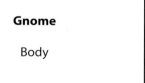

Gnome

Body

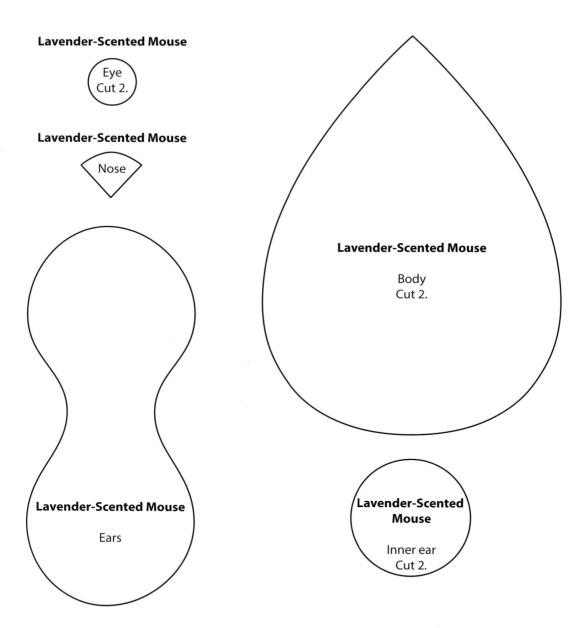

Lavender-Scented Mouse

Eye
Cut 2.

Lavender-Scented Mouse

Nose

Lavender-Scented Mouse

Ears

Lavender-Scented Mouse

Body
Cut 2.

Lavender-Scented Mouse

Inner ear
Cut 2.

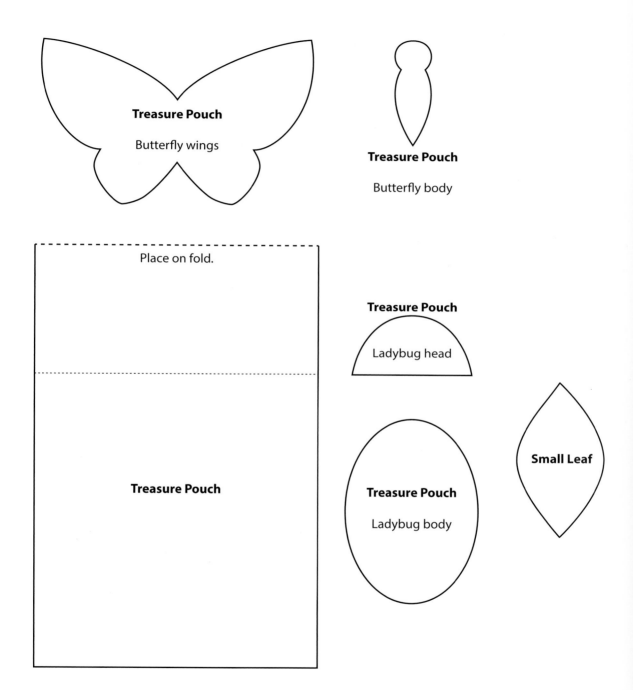

Treasure Pouch

Butterfly wings

Treasure Pouch

Butterfly body

Place on fold.

Treasure Pouch

Treasure Pouch

Ladybug head

Treasure Pouch

Ladybug body

Small Leaf

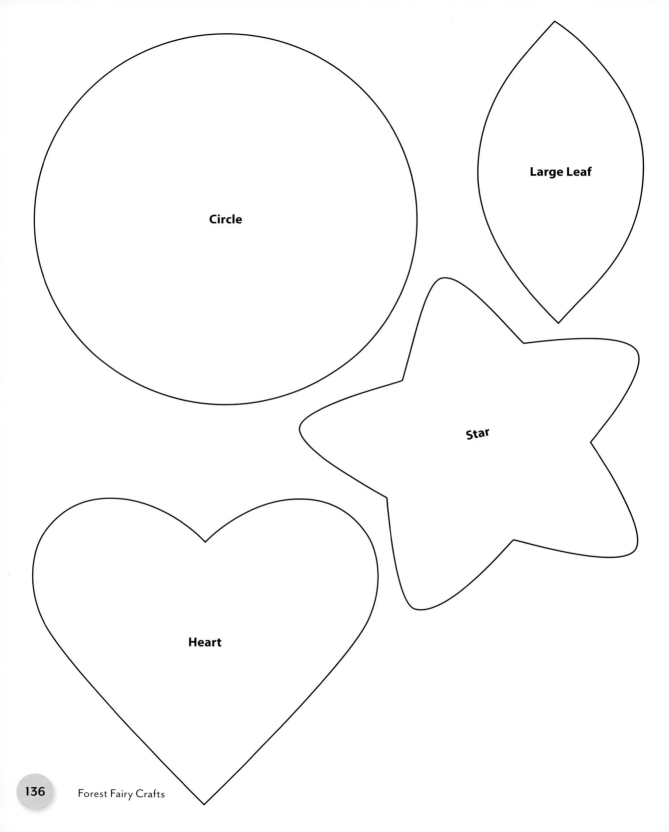

Circle

Large Leaf

Star

Heart

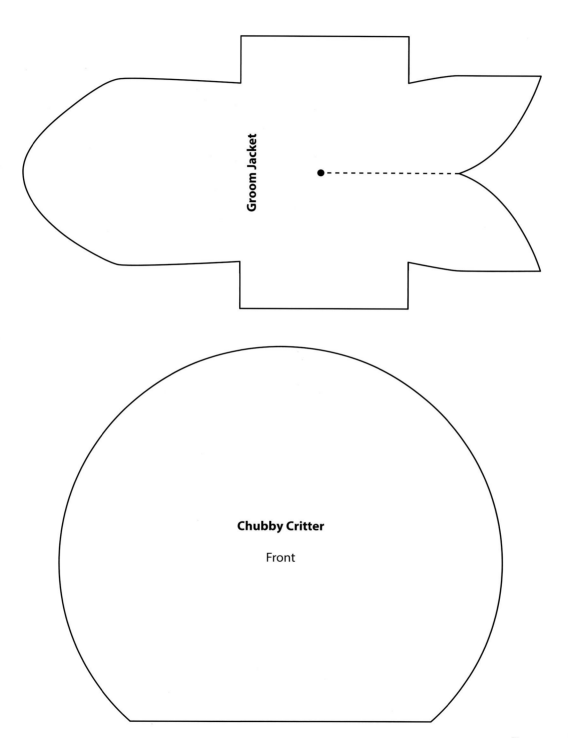

Groom Jacket

Chubby Critter

Front

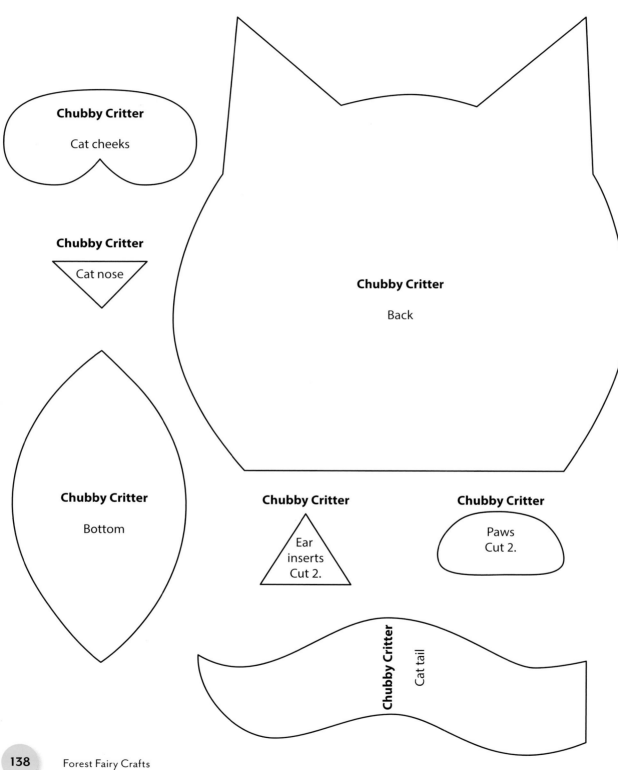

Chubby Critter

Cat cheeks

Chubby Critter

Cat nose

Chubby Critter

Back

Chubby Critter

Bottom

Chubby Critter

Ear
inserts
Cut 2.

Chubby Critter

Paws
Cut 2.

Chubby Critter

Cat tail

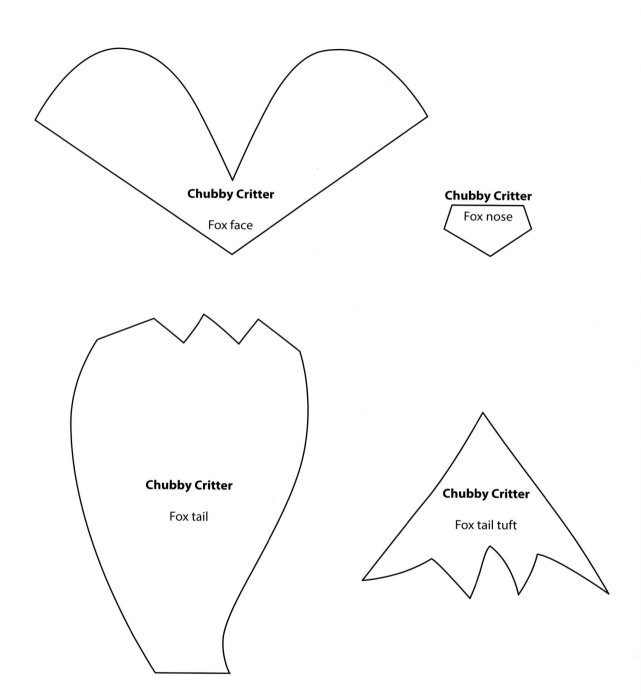

Chubby Critter

Fox face

Chubby Critter

Fox nose

Chubby Critter

Fox tail

Chubby Critter

Fox tail tuft

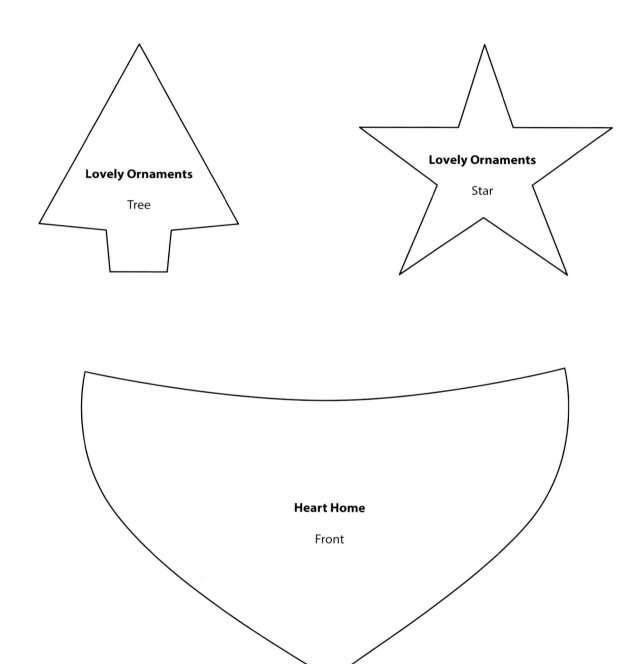

Lovely Ornaments

Tree

Lovely Ornaments

Star

Heart Home

Front

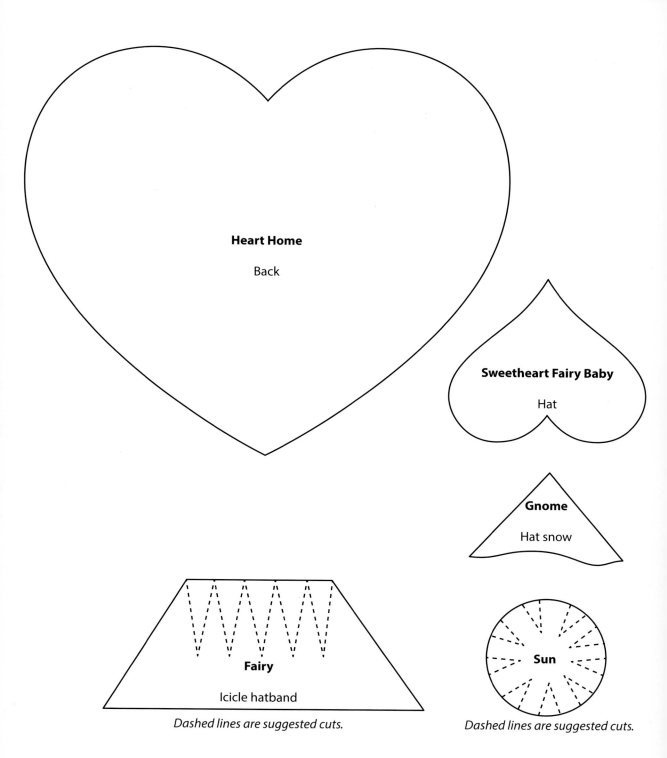

Heart Home

Back

Sweetheart Fairy Baby

Hat

Gnome

Hat snow

Fairy

Icicle hatband

Dashed lines are suggested cuts.

Sun

Dashed lines are suggested cuts.

Every season has beauty and magic waiting to be discovered. Explore the world with fairy crafts.

About the Authors

Photo by Lenka Vodicka-Paredes

LENKA AND ASIA live in the foothills of Northern California. They started making toys for their children and then taught fairy-making and sewing crafts to students at the Nevada City School of the Arts. Since the publication of the their first book, *Forest Fairy Crafts*, they have delighted in seeing their ideas come to life all around the world. They enjoy making fairies with their children, Asia's granddaughter, and a fluffy black-and-white dog named Chewbacca, who chews on fairy bead heads when he can reach them.

Follow Lenka and Asia on social media:

Website: forestfairycrafts.com

(Make sure to check out their blog!)

Want even more creative content?

Make it, snap it, share it
using
#ctpublishing